UP

ALSO BY BEN FOGLE

English

Land Rover

Labrador

The Accidental Naturalist

The Accidental Adventurer

BEN FOGLE
& MARINA FOGLE

UP

MY LIFE'S JOURNEY TO
THE TOP OF EVEREST

WILLIAM
COLLINS

William Collins
An imprint of HarperCollins*Publishers*
1 London Bridge Street
London SE1 9GF
WilliamCollinsBooks.com

First published in Great Britain by William Collins in 2018

22 21 20 19 18 17
10 9 8 7 6 5 4 3 2 1

A catalogue record for this book is
available from the British Library

HB ISBN 978-0-00-831918-2
TPB ISBN 978-0-00-831919-9

Printed and bound in Great Britain by
CPI Group (UK) Ltd, Croydon, CR0 4YY

MIX
Paper from
responsible sources
FSC   FSC® C007454
www.fsc.org

This book is produced from independently certified FSC paper
to ensure responsible forest management.

For more information visit: www.harpercollins.co.uk/green

To the Sherpa people,
the real heroes of the mountain

CONTENTS

TIMELINE

13/4/18 – ARRIVAL KATHMANDU

14/4 – LUKLA (2,800 metres)

15/4 – NAMCHE BAZAAR (3,400 metres)

16/4 – TRAIL TO PANGBOCHE (4,100 metres)

17/4 – PUJA CEREMONY, PANGBOCHE MONASTERY
(with Lama Nawang Pal)

18/4 – TRAINING CLIMB (to 5,000 metres)

19/4 – CLIMBERS' MEMORIAL, LOBUCHE (4,950
metres)

20/4 – KHUMBU VALLEY

21/4 – BASE CAMP

26/4 – RETURN TO BASE CAMP AFTER ASCENT TO LHOTSE FACE ABOVE CAMP 2 (6,400 metres)

30/4–3/5 – ROTATION TO CAMP 3 (7,200 metres)

4/5 – VIC LEAVES

7/5 – TRAINING HIKE

8/5 – SCHOOL ASSEMBLY SATELLITE CALL

16/5 – 7.30 AM EVEREST SUMMIT (8,800 metres)

18/5 – LEAVE BASE CAMP FOR HOME

AN END AND A BEGINNING

Dear Ludo and Iona,

Life is about the journey not the destination.
*Live it brightly. Live it brilliantly and live it wisely. Don't
    waste it. Not one single day.*
Add life to your days not days to your life.

Dream.
Dare.
Do.
Live for the now, not the then.

Be spontaneous.
Smile.
Go with your heart. Instinct is often right.
Take criticism on the chin and use it usefully.

Life is there to complete, not to compete. Although it will
    sometimes feel like a competition, don't get swept up by it.
    It's not a race.
Be magnanimous in victory and graceful in defeat.
Be humble and try not to grumble.

Confide. Don't divide.
Reach don't preach.
Be caring and considerate.
Be principled but open-minded enough to be pragmatic.

Try and be the shepherd not the sheep.
Remember, you aren't just a face in the crowd. You're
    unique.
Despite a planet of seven billion. There is no one else like
    you.

Your personality will be shaped and moulded by the
    company you keep and the experiences you have.
Be comfortable with who you are. Don't try and be what
    others want or expect you to be.

Listen, be curious and learn.
Wealth is all about how YOU interpret it. Money will not
    buy you happiness nor love.
Experiences WILL make you richer.
Travel will broaden your mind.

People will judge you, but don't let that judgement define you.
Don't let failure defeat you.
Insecurity will creep up on you throughout life, try not to
    listen to it.
Be confident, never arrogant.
Give.
Share.

People will be outrageous and provocative. Try not to be
    outraged or provoked.
Don't live life through a screen. Live it for bikes and hikes,
    not likes and swipes.
Routine is far more dangerous than risk.

Some days you will feel a little down. The highs and lows are
    human nature.
Your life should be filled with light and shade, it is these ups
    and downs that remind us what is important in life.

Fortune really does favour the brave.

Be brave.
Take risks.
Live your life.
Smile.

And don't forget to look UP.

Love Daddy

Ring ring … ring ring … ring ring …

It's 4 am and I'm in a hotel room in Toronto, Canada. I'm here for my grandmother's 100th birthday. Her 100th birthday! I still marvel at that. I cancelled everything to be here for this, including leaving my family in Austria.

I hate calls in the night. They make me nervous. They are almost always bad. No one calls with good news at 4 am. Maybe it's a wrong number. My heart is pounding.

'It's Dad,' says the voice on the line. He's in the room next door. Why is he calling me?

'Marina has lost the baby.'

I struggle to comprehend what he is telling me. I only left Marina yesterday, eight months pregnant and healthy, while I flew to Canada.

And why is *he* telling me this? I look at my mobile. It's switched off.

'It's not good, she might not make it either, you've got to get back.'

My world imploded. It's funny how we never realise how happy and lucky we are until it's gone. I had the perfect, happy life and in that single phone call I saw the happiness disappear. It was like a little bomb going off in my life.

Not only had I lost a baby that I had been longing to meet, but I also faced the reality of losing my beloved wife, Marina. My soul mate, my best friend and the mother to my children.

I wasn't ready to become a widower.

The next 12 hours are a bit of a blur. By the time I had thrown on some clothes, Dad had booked me a plane ticket to London. I raced to the airport and was on a flight by 6 am.

It was the worst flight of my life. And I've had some bad flights.

For eight long hours, I would have no contact with the outside world. I sat in my seat and imagined what was happening. My sister-in-law, Chiara, warned me in a call before my flight that Marina was bleeding so profusely that she might not make it. Please God, don't take her from me. I am not a religious person, but here I was, 30,000 feet up, calling on the heavens to hear my prayers.

I sat there with tears streaming down my face. How could I cope? I couldn't imagine life without Marina, the lynchpin of our family. The fun and the happiness. The glue. She was *the* family. We would be lost without her. The children, what about the children? What did they know? Ludo was four and Iona three. How would I tell them? How could I tell them?

My happy life flashed before my eyes during that endless flight. Our wedding in Portugal, the honeymoon in the Outer Hebrides, the family holidays, dancing in the kitchen. How could life ever be happy again? How could I go up from here?

As the plane touched down at Heathrow, I turned on my phone. How I was dreading this moment. Rain drizzled down the oval plane window as I called Chiara, who was still a further 1,000 miles away in Austria.

'She's still in intensive care … but they have stopped the bleeding … she's going to live.'

I burst into tears and jumped into a taxi to Luton where I caught a flight to Salzburg in Austria. Those 12 hours were like a foggy nightmare. It was like I was living someone else's life. This was the kind of thing that only happened to other people, not us.

In Salzburg, I can remember the shafts of bright light streaming through the hospital windows as I walked up the white corridor. I walked into a large room bathed in Alpine summer
sunshine, net curtains blowing in the gentle breeze from the open
windows. I could just make out the mountains in the distance. It
was ethereal. Beautiful and calming.

In the middle of the room was a bed surrounded by nurses in
starched white uniforms, their smiles dazzling. White. Bright.
Warm.

I walked over to the bed. Marina's blonde hair spilt over the
pillow, her face was drained of colour. Everything was white.
Clinical, but calm and soothing.

I held her hand and she opened her eyes. She smiled. I love her
smile, it's so beautiful. It's infectious. Tears rolled down my cheeks.
She looked at me and squeezed my hand.

'Do you want to meet him?'

Him. My baby was a boy. We had deliberately not found out his
sex. Marina wanted to have a surprise, something to look forward
to at the end of labour. A boy, another little boy. A son.

Wait. What does she mean, *meet him*? I knew he had been
stillborn.

'I think we should meet him to say goodbye.'

I like to think of myself as a pretty stable, well-prepared individual, little surprises me and I am rarely flummoxed. 'Expect the
unexpected' has always been my mantra; but now, here, in this
faraway hospital in a strange land, I was being invited to meet and
to hold my dead son.

One of the nurses appeared with a baby blanket. She held it in
her arms gently and walked through the shafts of sunlight. My

heart raced. Nothing, I mean nothing in my life had prepared me for this.

She handed me the little bundle. I cupped him in my arms and peered at his little face. He was so beautiful. He looked like he was asleep.

'What shall we call him?' Marina smiled.

'I think we should call him Willem.' Tears splashed onto his little cheeks.

Here was a little boy I had longed to meet but would never get to know. For eight months, I had imagined a complete family of five. Suddenly, those dreams had been shattered.

It can be difficult for those who haven't experienced this unique form of bereavement to understand how painful it can be, to lose someone you never knew, but I felt like I was suffocating.

I stared at little Willem and made a resolution there and then that I would live the rest of my life for the two of us, that I would relish every day. I would always smile. I would live it to its full. For little Willem, I would live my life even more brightly, seizing the moments and the opportunities and pursuing my dreams.

Little did I know it, but in that dreadful moment of tragedy and disappointment was the germ of a journey that would turn my life around and lead me up to the top of the world.

Up.

'Always look Up,' my late grandmother used to say. It was good advice. It is too easy to go through life looking down.

It is almost a symptom of modern society, to look down, both physically and metaphorically. Travel on the commuter train, bus or tube each morning and they are full of people looking down. Down at their phones, their newspapers, their feet, anywhere but up, for fear of making eye contact. Walk along most streets and they are full of people looking down at their phones, their feet, the pavement.

It is like we have evolved into a downward-looking species.

I remember once on a visit to New York, a taxi driver pointed out that he could always spot a tourist because they were the ones looking up. That observation is so symbolic. You see, to New Yorkers, those magnificent vertiginous skyscrapers were just another part of their landscape. Complacency meant they never looked up and admired the city that others flocked to.

Can you imagine how much we miss out on by looking down? Those chance encounters, opportunities and sights. To my mind, we have become an increasingly pessimistic, negative and angry society. We have become suspicious of success. Social media and the press will often pick on the negative, downward-facing stories and opinions.

Where is the Up? The positivity, the optimism and the celebration? I'm sure if more people looked up and smiled, we would be in a happier world.

If there is one thing I encourage my children to do, it is to smile. Not in a needless, fake kind of way, but in a positive karma kind of way. A smile has a natural way of lightening and lifting the head.

Take a look around you. Downward-facing frowns? Lift your head and smile.

INTRODUCTION

It was a hot summer's afternoon in 2016 and I was in a crowded tent at Goodwood House in Sussex. My wife Marina and I had been invited by Cartier to join them for lunch at the Festival of Speed. I made my way to our table and peered at the name card next to me.

Victoria Gardner.

I'd never heard of her, which was just as well, as she wasn't there.

Thirty minutes passed and, after I'd finished my starter, a young girl appeared, apologised profusely for her lateness and sat in the chair next to me.

I recognised her instantly: Victoria Pendleton, the heroine of British cycling. Two-time Olympic gold medallist and umpteen-time world champion. I was dizzy with excitement. I had followed her career closely and admired her ability to excel at sport while not becoming a slave to it. I had always liked the way she spoke her mind and appeared to ruffle feathers by breaking convention. I admired her individuality in a sport with a reputation for unquestioning conformity.

I had long thought that Victoria would make a great adventuring companion if ever I met her. For several hours, we chatted. I told her that if ever she wanted to embark on an expedition or an adventure, I would love to explore some ideas. Without hesitation, she accepted, and in the inauspicious and unlikely surroundings of that marquee, we hatched a plan that would take us to one of the wildest, most dangerous places on earth, on a journey that would change our lives forever.

For several years, I had been travelling the world to spend time with people who had abandoned the conformity of society and followed their dreams into the wilderness. Each one had inspired me to do more with my own life, but each time I found myself returning home and plugging back into our 'vanilla' society. Safe. Risk averse. Conforming. Restricting. Angry.

I have always wanted more. I have always wanted to shake the manacles of expectation. Over the years, I have dipped in and out of it, but I have always returned to the safety of home and complacency.

I had been looking for something to shake my foundations and reconnect me with the wilderness.

The modern world is a complex one. Aged 44, I sometimes worry I can't keep up with it. Technology and communication have advanced at breakneck speed. Never have we been bombarded with so much information. Never has society been held up to such scrutiny.

What's more, we have become increasingly polarised. World politics is the manifestation of our fractured society. You are either in or out. For or against. Yes or no. Up or down.

Negativity is a blight on society. It might just be the rose-tinted retrospective reflection of my childhood, but I'm sure when I was younger everything was more positive. Negativity was the realm of Eeyore, the donkey from *Winnie-the-Pooh*. Eeyore was in the minority with his pessimism and gloom.

Today, there seems to be a bubbling undertone of resentment and anger that is contagious. It seems to manifest itself in this fast-paced, downward-looking burden. But it doesn't have to be that way.

You can live your life Up.

I have always tried to look Up. That doesn't mean I haven't looked back, far from it, we can all learn a great deal from our past. From the highs and lows, the good decisions and the bad. The successes and the mistakes.

You see, looking Up has become something bordering on the spiritual. I am not religious, but that doesn't mean I don't look up.

'Do you believe in God?' asked my son Ludo one morning.

'I don't know,' came the answer that surprised me. I'd probably describe myself as an atheist. I'm open-minded. I've been into the various churches of God over the years. I don't have a particular calling to a specific 'god' per se, but that is not to say I don't believe in a higher calling.

It's just that mine is a little wilder. The wilderness is my religion. Nature. The flora and fauna. It is my church. I feel the same connection to a higher being when in the wilderness as many do in a church. My god is not specific. It's the trees and the mountains and the rivers and the waterfalls. The wilderness heals; it soothes and calms.

Don't worry, I'm not going to get too philosophical here, but it is important to understand my calling, because the wilderness in all her cloaks has a powerful spirituality. Of course, there are plenty of cultures who have long revered the sun and the moon and the power they have over us, and there are many pagans who also have a deep connection to the land and the earth.

Mine is less structured. It's difficult to define, but I find the wilderness has an almost magnetic pull over me and perhaps it is the reason for this story. The call of the wild has helped mould and shape me into the man I am today. My relationship with the wilderness has never been one of battle or war. It has never been Man versus nature, but Man *with* nature. I've tried to find the careful balance of harmony, of mutual respect, of collaboration.

We have such a complex relationship with nature. In some ways, we have tried to tame it and control it: look at our cities and townscapes. We have beaten nature into submission, sanitised it and suppressed it. It's almost as if we are terrified of it. Scared of its power over us.

I have never been fearful of the wilderness. Respectfully wary, and often humbled by it, but I've always loved being close to mother nature. She has a way of simplifying life.

Nature has the power to strip us back to our basic instincts. It's no wonder there are movements around the world for rehabilitation and therapy in the wilderness, to use the forests and the woods as a way of treating ill health.

Forest schools are increasing in popularity and many nations, from Japan to Norway, have become popular destinations for forest bathing, in which people lie on the forest floor and stare up at the canopy above.

There is already scientific evidence of the healing virtues of the flora and fauna around us. It has always been perfectly obvious to me that we have a closer affinity to water, trees and mountains than we do to skyscrapers, roads and cars.

It feels like we have the very basics of our existence upside down. Rather than living in the concrete, grey cityscape and 'escaping' to the countryside for holidays or breaks, we should live closer to nature and 'visit' the cityscapes.

Of course, cities hold the key to work and opportunity, but once again we seem to have our principles and priorities slightly skewed. Do we work to live, or live to work?

I have always been attracted to a hand-to-mouth existence. A small-scale subsistence lifestyle has always seemed more compelling than the intensity of the materialistic, commercialised culture in which most of us in the Western world have chosen to live. Connected to the grid, we are slaves to money. We must pay taxes, mortgages and fees. The governments rely on a working society to generate income and therefore tax.

For the last six years, I've been working on a TV series about people who have dropped out of society and started a new life disconnected from the state. They have cut themselves off from 'the grid', severed their connection to electricity, water, gas, phone and in some cases money.

For me, expeditions have been my own, short-term opportunity to live off the grid. Expeditions have given me a chance to test my resolve and pique my resourcefulness. When I'm back at home, a cultural lethargy envelops me. When something goes wrong with the electrics or the car or the drainage, I will, by default, call in someone else to help.

The fully functioning circular economy relies on everyone having a skill. We have become reliant on a collective taskforce in which we all have mono skills rather than the universal multi-tasking multi-skills of old.

My late grandfather built his own house on the shores of a Canadian lake. He dug the foundations, installed the pipework and the electrics. He cut the wood, roofed the house and fitted the windows.

I like to think of myself as a well-rounded individual, but I wouldn't know where to begin when it comes to building a house. I can sail, scuba dive and speak fluent Spanish, but I don't understand electrics and I can't even hammer a nail properly. Which set of skills are more useful? The latter of course; the problem is that society no longer requires them and we have lost the connection to our basic knowledge.

The wilderness requires resourcefulness; it forces us to connect with an inner self that once relied on survival skills to exist. When pushed, it's amazing how adaptable we can become. The problem is that so few of us ever get a chance to test ourselves. We tend to take the easy option and avoid hardship. For me, expeditions have always been a way of reconnecting with my inner wildman.

The first time I really challenged myself was when I was marooned for a year on a remote corner of a windswept, treeless island in the Outer Hebrides of Scotland. I had volunteered to be a castaway for a year on the island of Taransay, as part of a unique social experiment by the BBC to celebrate the millennium.

A group of 36 men, women and children were given 12 months to become a fully functioning community. We were given all the materials we would need to build accommodation, install water piping, a wind turbine and fencing. We put up polytunnels to grow fruit and veg in the inclement Scottish weather and we reared pigs, sheep and cattle. We built a slaughterhouse, harvested crops and became a simple, thriving off-grid community.

I learned so many new skills during that year: farming, building, teaching. In many ways, it converted a group of underskilled urbanites into a well-rounded, multi-tasking community, in which we all shared our different skill sets and knowledge for the betterment of the whole.

We became a very happy little settlement. I think we reintroduced lost values into our little community. We cared collectively for one another. There was no place for materialism. Our community was based on subsistence. We worked with what we had and maximised our efficiency. After 12 months, we were a happier, healthier, more efficient group of people.

In some ways, I have been chasing that beautiful, simple life ever since.

Castaway for a year on an island, rowing the Atlantic, trekking across Antarctica … all of these experiences have had a profound effect on me.

But it was Everest that changed me for good.

This seven-week expedition into the death zone was a life-changing, life-enhancing adventure. I walked the fine line between life and death. I experienced feelings and emotions that I'd never had before.

I never planned to write a book. After all, thousands of great mountaineering books have been written before. What would make my story so unique? Well, I hope you will read this book, not as an ego-chasing journey to the top of the world, but as a life-affirming lesson.

Humbled and enlightened, I hope these words jump out with the intensity of my own experience. I hope the positivity and the happiness and the joy overshadow the obligatory danger, fear and suffering that comes with a high-altitude mountain adventure.

I hope this book will inspire you to climb your own Everest.

CHAPTER ONE

FAMILY

We were on a deserted beach in the Caribbean when I proposed to Marina.

Over a picnic of tea and sandwiches, I got down and proposed with a ring made from a little piece of string. I had just spent two months rowing across the Atlantic Ocean and hadn't had time to get to a proper jewellers, so instead I made a special ring from a little piece of rope on the boat.

By the summer, we were married. I couldn't wait to start my own family, but we decided not to rush into parenthood. It would be several years until Marina fell pregnant for the first time.

I had never been happier. We waited until the 12-week scan to tell everyone. In anticipation, we invited friends and family over for a party. That afternoon, we went for the final scan only to discover there was no heartbeat. We had lost our little child before it had even had time to form. It was crushing, but Marina insisted on going ahead with the party – one of many episodes in our lives that shows her resilience.

A month later, I went to Antarctica with James Cracknell. The polar trek was a pretty good way to overcome the tragedy of the loss. For those who haven't experienced miscarriage, it can be a difficult thing to explain. To be honest, I had no idea of the emotional disappointment of losing a child at such a young age. It isn't so much the loss, as the loss of the dream.

For three months, we had dreamed and hoped and planned. Of course, all new parents are warned not to become too hopeful before the 12-week scan, but we were intoxicated by happiness and perhaps confident through hopeful arrogance. We'd be fine, we had assumed.

We survived, and it made us both stronger. Less than a year later, Marina was pregnant again and this time she carried to term until we gave birth to our first child, a little baby boy we called Ludo.

Ludo brought such joy and happiness into our lives. Overnight, this little screaming baby became our world. Parenthood can be pretty overwhelming. As dog owners, both Marina and I had been pretty sure we would find it easy. A dog is, unsurprisingly, very different to a baby. We lived through the fog of broken sleepless nights and slowly life became a little easier.

What surprised me most was my instinctive spirit to nest and protect. Inadvertently, I found myself being more careful. I worried more and became more risk averse.

I don't know if this is instinctive behaviour or whether it is born from the conventions of society, but I soon found fatherhood to be domineering, not in a bad way, but in an all-encompassing, all-consuming change to my lifestyle.

Ludo became our world. He was our everything. We were dazzled by the beauty of parenthood and that blinded us temporarily to everything else.

Family has always been important to me. I grew up in a tightly-knit family, the middle sibling to two sisters, living above my father's veterinary clinic. We were close to our extended family, too. My parents gently instilled the core values of family life and it is probably no surprise that we all live within a mile radius of one another in central London.

Fortunately for me, my wife is also from a very close family. Perhaps it was part of the attraction for me. As it happens, I probably now spend more time with her parents and sisters than with my own. We spend most weekends with them in their little cottage in Buckinghamshire and the summer with them in Austria.

Whenever I travel, I am always moved by the intensity of the family dynamic in other parts of the world. Almost every other country places the family at the heart of the nation. Grandparents, aunts, uncles all live together. The very concept of retirement homes or old people's homes is as alien as the concept of not putting family first. In Britain, I think family is a little more insular. For many it is the tight immediacy of the parents and their children. The wider family is often an afterthought for Christmas or a summer barbecue. The reason I never moved overseas permanently was because of the call of my family. I couldn't bear the thought of being so far from them all.

To become a parent myself gave me a whole new perspective on life. I now had the parental responsibilities. I had a little child that would rely on me for the next 20 years or so. I was responsible for caring, sharing and preparing this little boy for life.

I had to teach him what was right and what was wrong. What was good and what was bad. Love and hate. Fear and loss. I was overwhelmed at the incredible burden of responsibility. What if I got it wrong? What if I failed? Can you fail at being a father?

No amount of planning or preparation can really prepare you for the magnitude of the journey. You can't press the pause button. You can't change your mind. Fatherhood is an unstoppable expedition into the unknown.

Expedition isn't a bad way to describe it. You try to plan and prepare. It involves a whole new routine that often includes sleep deprivation and fear. It's like you enter a new world in which you're never really sure if you are right or wrong.

I felt guilty about taking even the shortest overseas assignments, which was at odds with my instinctive desire to feather my nest financially. Money had never been a priority; of course it is a powerful enabler, but I've always been happy with simplicity, and the desire to accumulate great wealth has never been an ambition.

Overnight, this relaxed attitude changed into a sort of panic. As a freelancer, I had no guarantee of work from one day to the next. The vulnerability of a TV presenter cannot be underestimated. Our value can plunge overnight in the blink of a single scandal or change of a commissioner. Fashions change, and with them presenters come and go. As Piers Morgan likes to say, 'One minute you are the cock of the walk, the next you are a feather duster.'

Most of all, I wanted to be a good role model. I admired, and still admire, both my parents. I am so proud of their achievements, and part of my own drive has been to make them equally proud. For me to succeed in life feels like success for them as parents.

Success isn't always about impressing other people, but how can you ever define success if there is no one to congratulate you?

It wasn't long before Marina was pregnant with our second child, Iona. Once again, we dipped into the nocturnal fog of parenthood, and once again I found myself torn by the contradiction of wanting to be a stay-at-home dad. To nurture and protect while at the same time battling my desire to build up my financial resources and work.

It was like trying to juggle too many balls. Family, friends, work, ambition and adventure. You can't have your cake and eat it. The problem was that adventure has always been at the heart of who I am, and while instinct drove me to nest build, passion for the pursuit of adventure was driving me closer and closer to Everest, my childhood dream.

For as long as I can remember, I have always wanted to climb her. The first time I remember seeing a photograph of Everest was in *National Geographic* magazine. It seemed so extraordinary that man, with all our advancement, had taken until 1953 to get to the top.

I spent hours staring at those photographs of the towering peak, of weathered faces and heroic sherpas. There was something so romantically mesmerising and alluring about her. Dangerous and beautiful. I found myself dreaming about her. Thinking about her. But it was always just that. A dream. Like the pretty girl at school, I was never going to get her. I wasn't a mountaineer. It seemed beyond my grasp on so many levels.

I'm not sure what it was that so captivated me. The remoteness. The romance of the highest place on earth. The drama. The tragedy. She has been at centre stage for so many incredible tales. Some heroic. Many tragic. Plenty unexplained.

As a young boy, summiting Everest represented the pinnacle of human endeavour. In my young mind, it was the ultimate achievement. It required grit, strength, bravery and confidence. None of which I had very much of, which is maybe why it had such magnetism. Here was a mountain that attracted the brave few; the romantics pursuing their standing at the top of the world.

Over the years, I had met plenty of people who had climbed Everest: Kenton Cool, Sir Ranulph Fiennes, Bear Grylls, Annabelle Bond, Jake Meyer, the list goes on. To be honest, I seemed to know more people who had climbed it than hadn't. I felt like the odd one out. It always made me feel like I had missed out on this incredible moment. Not in a 'bagging' or 'ticking off' kind of a way, but in the pursuit of my dream.

Many people are put off by the number of those who have climbed Everest. Nearly 4,000 have had the privilege of standing on the top of the world. I'd say out of a world population of over 7 billion, that's still quite small.

It is difficult to define 'why'. When Mallory was asked he famously answered, 'because it's there'. As flippant as it sounds, I can relate to his sentiments. We live in an age where there has to be a purpose and reason for everything we do.

There had never been a clear 'purpose' for me to climb Everest. In past conversations with Marina she had quite rightly explained that if climbing and mountaineering was my passion, then I should, and could quite justifiably, attempt a summit, but why? She had asked, why would I risk so much for so little?

Was I not risking my life to simply stand on a point? The answer is yes and no. For me, the Everest dream has always been so much more than just an ego trip. It's the whole thing. The trek to Base Camp. The Icefall. The Western Cwm, the Lhotse Face, the South Col, the Balcony, the Hillary Step. For me, having read countless books, these places have the same spiritual draw as a pilgrimage.

Everest has always represented everything I dream of achieving. It has always had a wild, dangerous romance that is at the same time both terrifying and electrifying. It fills me, has always filled me, with such wondrous fascination and appeal. Like a forbidden fruit. So close and yet so far. Within touching distance.

It's like an historian visiting the archaeological sites of the world, or a geographer visiting the geological sites.

I was wrestling with the balance between my need for adventure and my love of my family. Can you justifiably juggle both? Where is the line between sensible and selfish? I had found myself torn between the pursuit of my dreams and my family, who are my everything.

In the end, it comes down to who I am and what makes me who I am. Without travel, without adventure and without wilderness, I am nothing. Life is about embracing the good and the bad. It is the heady mix of fear, danger, adversity, heroics, romance, wilderness, beauty, tragedy, love, loss and achievement. Ultimately, it's about pursuing our dreams. To dare to do. To dare to go where others fear.

What more can you ask for in life?

Everest would give me all that. It was a gamble. It was risky. There were dangers, but if I wasn't being true to myself then how could I be honest to my own family? I just had to persuade Marina that climbing the highest mountain on earth was a good idea for all of us.

Marina – Home

For as long as I can remember, Ben has wanted to climb Everest. I guess, when you're in his line of work, wanting to scale the tallest mountain in the world should come as no surprise. But Ben is a dreamer and I'm a realist, and when he'd talked of his lofty ambition, I'd always pooh-poohed the idea, dismissing his dream.

It's not that I wasn't seduced by the world's tallest mountain in the way that he was. I grew up on a diet of adventure books. I spent my gap year reading the mountaineering authors Joe Simpson and Jon Krakauer. The ambitions of my 18-year-old self, aspirational and seemingly immortal, included participating in the Vendée Globe – the single-handed round-the-world sailing race – and climbing an 'eight-thousander', probably Everest, maybe even K2. As I waved Ben off from La Gomera on his mission to row the Atlantic, I was selecting which of my friends I'd ask to be in my team for the same race in two years' time.

What is more telling is that by the time he'd reached the other end and I'd realised just what such a challenge

*involved, the idea had been well and truly scrapped. With a
new ring on my finger and a wedding to organise, I was
delighted to be at Ben's side as he undertook his challenges.
As his wife I would have the best seat in the house, but there
was no way I was actually going to do them.*

*For Ben, however, actually participating in adventures is
part of his DNA. My bold spouse is always on the lookout for
a feat that will inspire the nation. When Ben announced he
was going to row the Atlantic, everyone looked at me
incredulously, not believing you could actually row across an
ocean that only the most hardy sail across.*

*In the first few years of our marriage, Ben dabbled with
extremes – facing the bitter cold walking to the South Pole
and enduring the intense desert conditions walking across
the Empty Quarter. Part of me was hoping that this thirst for
adventure would cease as our children started needing him
more. I was banking on the fact that he'd never get bored of
talking about the life he'd led up until this point, and that I
could continue to brush the 'E idea' under the carpet.*

*The first time I knew he was serious was on a Sunday
afternoon as we walked across the Chiltern hills. The lives of
new parents tend to revolve around their children, leaving
the parents little time for each other. We're at the stage where
every conversation is hijacked by an eight-year-old.*

*'But Mummy, won't you get put in prison if you kill that
traffic warden?'*

'Mummy, what is resting bitch face?'

*So last year, we made a conscious decision to try and
have an hour when we walk and talk, just the two of us,*

every weekend. Since Ben is away for most of the year, the reality is that these walks happen once a month. Not ideal but good enough (which as every parent knows, is the gold standard).

Spring was just casting her delicate fingers over the winter-hewn hills. Around us new life was emerging from the rich earth, and blossom buds were tentatively bursting from naked trees. 'So I think I've found a way to do Everest,' Ben started. I glanced at him and at that moment my stomach lurched, because for the first time I knew he really meant it.

Ben and I don't have the kind of relationship where he tells me what he's going to do. I'd never have signed up for that, but as a couple we're absolutely terrible at conflict and so, over the decade that we've been married, we have worked out how to tackle potentially sensitive conversations without it resulting in an argument. We don't always achieve this, but amazingly, this time it worked.

I'd been told by a therapist that potentially difficult conversations are best had while walking. Raising your heart rate is good for the body and mind, and the fact that you're looking ahead rather than looking intensely into each other's eyes takes the edge off it. As we dipped into the Hambleden Valley, he told me his plan; that Kenton Cool, the rock star of the climbing world, had agreed to guide him, that he'd found a sponsor so that we didn't have to re-mortgage our house. He told me about why he'd always wanted to do it and, while he recognised such a feat would always be dangerous, what he was planning to do to mitigate that risk.

We returned home, our cheeks red from the chilly spring breeze, the dogs exhausted and me understanding that Everest was now a reality.

There was only ever one contender when it came to who could help us achieve this dream: Kenton Cool. I had known Kenton for several years after we had met through a mutual friend, Sir Ranulph Fiennes. He had told me that should I ever decide to do some climbing, we should consider teaming up together. Five years passed before I gave him a call to ask if he would help Victoria and myself with our Everest dreams.

Kenton set out a two-year plan for our Everest attempt. Respect of the mountain and a dedication to the project would ensure we had the best chances of summiting. He wanted to break it up into three phases. The first would involve an Alpine expedition for Victoria to give her a feel for the mountains. After all, while I was still a relative novice when it came to mountain climbing, Victoria was a mountaineering virgin. Green. Once she had become familiarised, we would then head to Bolivia for a three-week training programme in the Andes. This would then be followed by more training in the European Alps, before the final stage which would be a pre-Everest expedition to Nepal.

Kenton is one of Britain's most respected mountaineers who has an astonishing 12 summits under his belt. His climbing formula has been tried and tested so, although it would mean a huge amount of time away from family and work, I was committed to the plan.

The idea behind the programme was to build up our confidence using crampons, ice axes, ropes and harnesses. By the time we reached Everest, they needed to be second nature. We had to move efficiently and safely. It would also give us a chance to familiarise ourselves with mountain living. Once again, while I had plenty of experience of camping in the wilderness, for Victoria this would be a whole new experience.

Finally, it would also give us two years to get to know one another properly. To understand one another and to recognise our behaviours. The idea being that by the time we reached Everest, we would be able to know when something wasn't right; we would understand the nuanced behavioural changes that may be a result of altitude sickness.

For someone who has embraced the slow life, I am quite an impatient person, and the two-year plan was a pretty big commitment. To be honest, it was probably tailored more towards Victoria's inexperience, but we were a team and I relished the time we spent together.

In 2017, tragedy struck our tiny corner of West London. Just a few hundred metres from our house, Grenfell Tower caught alight and took more than 70 lives with her – some were friends. This tight-knit community was torn apart. It is still hard to think about. We pass the charred remains of that tragic building every day and we think about those lives lost.

It turned our little community upside down, but in those awful days and weeks after the inferno, a team of volunteers from the British Red Cross descended on North Kensington. It was both terrible and beautiful to see the same vehicles I had seen so often in faraway lands, now parked on my own street.

When Nepal was devastated by an earthquake back in 2015, the Red Cross had been one of the first aid agencies on the scene. I had long admired the Red Cross and decided that if I was going to climb Mount Everest, it would be in support of their incredible, heroic efforts at home and abroad. The countless volunteers across the world who selflessly dedicate their lives to improving the lives of others is true heroism, way greater than standing on the summit of any mountain.

Marina had given the green light. Kenton had agreed to help us prepare for Everest. We had agreed to support the British Red Cross and Victoria was fully committed to the expedition.

Now all we had to do was learn how to climb.

CHAPTER TWO

PREPARATION

After a long summer in the Austrian Alps, I left Marina and the children and headed to the other side of the world, to La Paz in Bolivia, where our team would have a crash course in mountain climbing. Kenton had designed an expedition that would take us up four Andean peaks in ascending order, culminating in Illimani at just under 6,500 metres (or three-quarters of the height of our ultimate goal, Everest).

I had only met Victoria a handful of times, and although I had known Kenton for a few years, we were all comparative strangers. This would be a great opportunity to get to know one another, and also to see if we were suited to mountains.

I had made it very clear to Victoria that she had to be 100 per cent sure that she wanted to take on the highest mountain in the world. I knew the risks involved. Everest required respect and commitment. The two-year plan we had embarked on would take us away from families and work for long stretches, so we had to both be fully invested. I felt a sense of responsibility that would be mitigated by Victoria's full commitment and devotion to the expedition. While mine was a childhood dream to climb Everest, hers was more about the 'challenge'.

It was early morning when we landed in the highest capital city in the world, La Paz. At 4,000 metres, it is so high that emergency oxygen cylinders are provided around the airport for new arrivals struggling with the thin air.

Our little minibus hurtled through the empty streets. La Paz really is an astonishing city. In the bowl of a valley, it is surrounded by towering snow-capped peaks. We explored the city for a day or two to acclimatise, even visiting the Witches' market with its dried llama foetuses, snakes, herbs and spells. There is something rather overwhelming in the enduring practice of witchcraft and folklore remedies.

We left the city for the peace and tranquillity of Lake Titicaca, the highest navigable lake in the world. I had first come here as a 19-year-old. I never forgot the haunting beauty of the lake with its floating reed islands and the fishermen's iconic boats. We spent a day sailing the lake on a reed boat, stopping at the Island of the Sun for an afternoon hike. Slowly, the three of us were getting to know our different personalities and discovering how we might work as a team: Kenton, the slightly laid back and forgetful mountain guide (so forgetful he had failed to pack a headtorch and a satellite phone for the final peak); Victoria, the vegan and ex-Olympian; and me, the romantic daydreamer.

On the face of it, we were a pretty unusual trio.

Our first summit to tackle was in the Cordillera Real, a mountain range situated a couple of hours from La Paz, where we hiked to base camp. For Victoria, it was her first proper camping experience. Not only was she learning the new art of mountaineering and acclimatising to the thin air, but she was also a camping virgin. On top of this was the difficulty in catering for a vegan in meat-loving, milk-drinking South America, where the local idea of a vegetarian is having half a portion of meat.

It had been many years since I climbed in crampons with ropes and harness. It was like becoming a student again as Kenton taught us the basics of rope work and how to plant our crampons in the ice. Testament to my climbing inexperience were the tattered, torn hems of my climbing trousers, where the sharp blades of the crampons had slashed through the material.

For 10 days we yomped, trekked, hiked and climbed across the Andean peaks until we reached our final challenge, Illimani. Victoria had struggled with the food and had been suffering from an upset stomach, but Kenton felt confident that we had the strength, stamina and resolve for our first 6,500-metre peak. After all, this was the main event. This was what we had come halfway around the world for. Leaving without an ascent would not only have felt like failure but also bad karma for our ultimate goal, Everest – more than two vertical miles higher.

I was halfway up the mountain when I got the call from Dad.

'It's Mum,' he said. 'She's in the ICU in an induced coma.'

The call came as a bolt from the blue. Why now, when I was stuck on the other side of the world?

I felt as helpless as I was clueless. I didn't know what to do. My instinct was to drop everything and head home as quickly as possible, but that was easier said than done when you are clinging to an icy mountain in the isolated nation of Bolivia.

Dad explained that Mum had fallen ill after a routine injection. The needle had pierced an artery and she had bled internally for 12 hours until she passed out. The hospital had placed her in an induced coma. She had a tracheostomy tube cut into her neck and she was in the intensive care unit, being cared for by four nurses, day and night.

'I'm coming home,' I told Dad.

'There's nothing you can do,' he reassured me, 'she's unconscious, she won't even know who's there.'

If all went well, we would summit the following day and I would be home within three days.

'She would want you to continue,' he added.

It was a knife-edge decision. My instinct was to head straight home, but even I could see the pointlessness of returning to a mother who was in an induced coma. Things weren't good, but Dad's reassuring tone implied that she was in the best hands and that three days wouldn't make a difference. I still don't know if I made the right decision, but I decided to carry on. Dad had implored me. He told me it was what Mum would have wanted me to do.

At midnight, we packed up our rucksacks and headed off for our first big summit together. Under torchlight we trudged and zig-zagged up the snowy, icy flanks of Illimani. She was a brute to climb. Starved of oxygen, cold and hungry, we battled on until dawn when the mountain was illuminated pink. The power of that sunrise was incredible. I could feel the sun charge my energy – it felt like new batteries had been placed inside me.

The three of us marched on in silence. Heads bowed to the mountain, each of us in our own misery. The suffering on a high mountain is largely invisible. It is the nakedness of that suffering that makes it harder to grasp. You end up hating yourself and beating yourself up for feeling as you do.

It is completely unlike running a marathon in which the physical drain is obvious. Here, the exhaustion is invisible. It creeps up on you and renders you useless. It is impossible to fight it; you simply have to endure it. Suffer it and deal with it.

'That's it,' came an exclamation from Victoria, 'I'm out.'

It was 6.30 am and we were just a few metres from the summit. Kenton and I were incredulous. She had endured more than six hours of climbing and hardship, only to declare her quitting a matter of minutes from the summit. It was as unexpected as it was illogical, but then mountains have a strange effect on people. Irrationality is the norm and unreasonable behaviour becomes commonplace. It is one of the reasons solo mountaineering is so dangerous. Without another perspective, it's difficult to gauge right from wrong. Kenton's surprise soon turned to exasperation.

'Get some bloody food in you,' he berated her. 'You have no energy because you haven't eaten anything.'

She had 'bonked', as the cycling term refers to it. She had used up her reserves and was running on empty. Kenton was right, but I could tell she didn't like his style. Victoria is not at all precious, but she has also spent her post-Olympic years trying to exorcise the ghosts of always being told what to do. She popped some nuts into her mouth and less than 20 minutes later we summited the highest peak that Victoria or I had ever climbed.

The summit was bittersweet. We had succeeded, but my mind and focus were elsewhere, back in Britain, worrying about my mother. The expedition had also opened a slight rift between Victoria and Kenton.

I spent the next few months visiting my mother's bedside each day. Slowly, she recovered and three months later she was discharged from hospital. She had defied the odds, and not only could she walk – something my father had warned us might not be possible – but she also had control of all her senses.

Meanwhile, Victoria was worried about the expedition. She had been unimpressed with Kenton's slightly laissez-faire approach. His lack of headtorch and failure to pack a satellite phone had rankled her. It had bothered me too, but I'd put it down to a one-off error.

Victoria is a harsher critic and I had to try and convince her that not only was Kenton still the man for the job, but also that Everest was still the right challenge for us.

We had both struggled in Bolivia. Victoria had displayed worrying physiological stats and had struggled in the thin air at 6,500 metres, the same height as Camp 1 on Everest. We would be going several vertical miles higher.

Bolivia had been my first real mountain test. It had pushed me physically, but I had also been inadvertently pushed mentally – worrying about both Victoria and my mother. I am a worrier. I wish I wasn't, but I am. I worry about everything. Worry and guilt are my two worst traits.

I'm one of those people that never really enjoys a party I host, because I'm so busy worrying about whether my guests are having a good time and guilty that they have made the effort to come to the party in the first place.

I often feel guilty. There is often no sensible or rational reason for it. I had always been worried (there we go again) that I would worry about Victoria. I felt a guilty responsibility for her being in the mountains in the first place, even though our decision to try and climb Everest had been very much a collaborative one.

Taking on Mount Everest was a massive task. We had to want it, but we also had to enjoy it. There was no point taking two years out of our lives, and the sacrifices that come with that, to climb one of the most dangerous mountains in the world, if we didn't really enjoy it.

Life is way too short to spend that amount of time doing something you aren't really committed to. I got the impression that Victoria had already dedicated enough of her life to cycling, which had never really been her passion. She had simply gone with the ride and discovered she was pretty good at it. She had impressed Kenton with her stamina and mental drive in Bolivia, but she hadn't impressed herself. We had both seen her ability to beat herself up. But I wanted Victoria to persevere. I could see the life-changing beauty that lay ahead for her, if only she would embrace the challenge.

Our second training expedition would take us into the heart of Nepal and the Himalayas. Kenton wanted to get us used to the high mountains of the Everest region, to introduce us to the food, the sherpas, the equipment and the landscape in which we would spend upwards of two months in our ultimate quest.

It was early January 2018. Kenton and Victoria had gone ahead of me. I thought it would be good for the pair of them to have an extra week to re-bond and connect. We needed absolute trust and confidence in one another, and it was the perfect opportunity for the two of them to spend time together.

I joined them a week later, at the foot of Imja Tse, a 6,000-metre snow peak in the Himalayas of eastern Nepal that is popular with trekkers. It was given the name 'Island Peak' by members of the 1953 British Mount Everest expedition, because it is surrounded by a sea of ice. Renamed Imja Tse some 20 years later, it is still called Island Peak by most trekkers and climbers today.

I had spent the previous month at sea-level with my family in the Bahamas. The cold, snowy mountains of Nepal were certainly a shock to the system as I helicoptered from Kathmandu deep into the Khumbu Valley – on the route to Everest herself. Within a day of arriving we were at base camp getting ready to climb another 6,000-metre peak. It was the first time since Bolivia that the three of us had been together in the mountains.

At midnight, we pulled on our safety harness and roped ourselves together. Joining us was a local sherpa called Siddhi. In the chill morning air, we set off up the mountain. The climb was easier than Illimani, but nonetheless we struggled.

About halfway up, Victoria stopped for a rest and she broke. She hit the wall and just couldn't go on. I was confused and upset, and I didn't know what we could do. If she was struggling here, then what would happen once we went higher?

Victoria settled on a safe glacial plane while the three of us climbed on towards the summit. We could see her all the way to the top, a tiny silhouette dwarfed by the surrounding snow and ice. Just as the summiting of Illimani had been tempered by worry and guilt, I found myself once again torn between the elation of reaching the summit of Island Peak, getting another step closer to my dream to climb Mount Everest, and my worry over Victoria.

Surprisingly, we never talked about what happened on Island Peak. I'm not sure why. In some ways, I assumed Victoria might have decided to abandon the expedition, but she didn't. In fact, she seemed to have a renewed sense of determination and Kenton and I admired her resolve.

An astonishing athlete, Victoria had embraced mountaineering effortlessly. I never doubted her physical ability and in fact, I always felt she had a better chance of summiting Everest than I did. But I could see that she struggled with self-doubt. She seemed to listen to a loud inner voice of negativity, which belied her strengths and amazing potential. Kenton and I did our best to reassure her and reinforce how good she was on the mountain, but her own questions about her ability were never far from her mind.

I asked her once whether she had ever been happy with her performance in life.

'No,' she replied.

'Not even when you won a gold medal?'

'I could have won it better,' she smiled back.

That's the thing about Victoria, always scrutinising herself, her own harshest critic.

I hoped that Everest would be a chance to change that. To embrace the unknown and the uncontrollable variables, to give in to the wilderness and silence the inner voice of doubt. We returned to Britain with just a couple of months to make final preparations for the climb.

Shortly after returning from Nepal, my father-in-law announced that after 40 years as a doctor, he had decided to retire. Weekly tennis and golf had kept him in rude health. Fit as a fiddle, he was in great shape. I had been thinking about the trek to Everest Base Camp and decided to invite both my father, Bruce and my father-in-law, Jonathan Hunt. Although I knew the trek would be demanding of two 70-year-olds, I also thought it would be a great opportunity for them to share the experience.

Both Mum and Dad had joined me in various escapades around the world. Dad came out to Ecuador and we visited the Galapagos together, and my mother came out to see me in Costa Rica where we explored the rainforest and even trekked to a smouldering volcano together. They had both come out to La Gomera when James Cracknell and I had set off to row across the Atlantic together, and they had been in Antigua when we arrived two months later.

They have both always supported me 100 per cent. I hate to think of the angst through which I must have put my mother.

In 2017, I invited Dad to join me in Tanzania. He had never visited Africa and I wanted to share with him the wonders of the Serengeti where I was making a documentary about the migration of the wildebeest as they made their way up to the Maasai Mara in Kenya. Dad was with us for 10 days, and it was magical to share with him one of my favourite places on earth.

Dad, at 74, is still working. A veterinary surgeon, he is one of the world's leading authorities on animal behaviour. He has written nearly a hundred books on dogs and cats and he *loves* his job. I have often worried about him and wondered whether retirement would be a sensible option, but then his job is who he is. I don't know what he would do without it.

Dad's commitment to the clinic and his continuing support of my mother, who was still convalescing at home after her long period in ICU, meant that he couldn't come on our Everest expedition, but Jonathan surprised me by accepting.

It had been a genuine offer and I hoped that he would add an extra dimension to the trek to Base Camp. While many people are drawn to the Base Camp trek itself, for us it was merely a means to an end. It was an important part of our acclimatisation, but it was incidental.

Kenton had warned us of the risk of sickness and ill health along the route. The 10-day trek to Base Camp is often the breeding ground for illness that can jeopardise the whole mountain climb, from colds and flu bugs to stomach ailments and other lurgies. Jonathan's 40-year career as a GP meant that we would have a doctor along with us to keep us in good health, as well as me having a family member there. He could be our team doctor.

Victoria and Kenton embraced the idea, and before we knew it, I found myself shopping with my father-in-law for pee bottles and thermal leggings. While having Jonathan along was a great idea, I was worried about the responsibility of taking him. The trek to Base Camp would be a relative walk in the park for those of us heading higher, but for a 70-something the trek could be physically demanding. What if something happened?

I knew how much it meant to Marina for him to accompany us. In a strange way I think it softened her overall worries. The original plan was that Jonathan accompany us to Base Camp where he could stay for a couple of days before heading home.

'I think he should stay for the whole expedition,' she said, 'why doesn't he become your Base Camp doctor too?'

I think there was a relief for Marina in the knowledge that we would both look out for one another. It made the Everest Expedition more palatable to her.

At the end of our Island Peak climb in Nepal, Victoria and I stayed on to do a couple of days' fieldwork with the Red Cross. The idea was we would visit some of the people and places supported by the charity.

On the first day, we visited a prosthetic clinic where those who had lost limbs in the earthquake had new limbs fitted. We watched a wheelchair basketball match and met survivors of the disasters, including a young boy who had lost his mother and his leg. We met volunteers who had lost family members and families who had lost their homes and their livelihoods. We visited a blood bank, where I left a pint of my own blood, and we visited rural communities that had lost all their infrastructure.

Victoria and I saw how the Red Cross had helped the Nepalese get back on their feet. They had helped communities rebuild water supplies and sanitation. We were shown how micro-financing had helped families start new businesses and stand on their own two feet. It was moving and humbling. For Victoria in particular, it gave purpose and meaning to our climb and strengthened her resolve. I was always worried that she didn't have the same motivation to climb Everest that I had.

While my ambition and hope were part of a lifelong dream, her motivation was slightly more rudderless. By that, I don't mean she lacked commitment, but I always felt she needed more of a reason why she should do it aside from just the physical challenge. Our time with the Red Cross in Nepal was surprisingly emotional and armed us both with a greater sense of purpose and connection to the task at hand.

CHAPTER THREE

RESPONSIBILITY

I hate goodbyes. I always have. And this one wasn't going to be easy.

The first goodbye I can remember was when I was about eight. My Canadian father would pack my two sisters and me off to his homeland every summer for eight weeks with my grandparents, Morris and Aileen. How I loved those long summers, those two months on the shores of Lake Chemong in the Kawartha region of Ontario in my grandfather's hand-built cottage. We paddled, swam and fished. It was the antithesis to London where we lived just off Baker Street in a house with no garden.

Here, nature was on our doorstep. We had freedom within the Canadian wilderness. I felt alive. But all good things must come to an end, and I'd have to say goodbye to Grandma and Grandpa for a year. I *hated* those goodbyes. I would bawl my eyes out when we were on the way to the airport and cry all the way back to England.

It's strange but 35 years later I can still feel the emotion, that unique pain of longing and missing. I'm sure it's why I still hate goodbyes.

Then there was the first time my mother dropped me off at boarding school. I was 14, a year later than everyone else mainly because I was never meant to go to boarding school. I didn't want to go. My parents didn't want me to go, but no other school would have me. My parents had taken the decision at an early age to send me to a private school, but I wasn't academic enough for the high-intensity academia of London day schools. I flunked my exams and ended up with a place boarding in Dorset.

The memory of Mum and Dad driving up the seemingly endless drive towards the imposing building will never fade. All the other pupils already knew one another. I was the new kid. Geeky, unsporty and spotty. I clung to my parents and cried for the better part of a year. *A year.* Can you imagine what I put my parents through? Sorry Mum and Dad.

Like I say, I've never been good at goodbyes and that hasn't changed.

We are in Colombo International Airport in Sri Lanka. We have just had the most amazing family holiday. Me, Marina, Ludo and Iona: three weeks exploring this beautiful Indian Ocean island. We have laughed and smiled, swum and surfed in the sweltering heat, met elephants and released baby turtles, bumped around in tuk-tuks and eaten every meal together. And now it's over.

I always get post-holiday blues, but this is different. Much, much different. It's bigger and it's sadder. I am saying goodbye as

I head off on the biggest challenge of my life. From here, I will fly straight to Kathmandu in Nepal while the rest fly back to England. Our happy family will separate, and I will begin a two-month expedition to climb the highest mountain in the world.

The last day in Colombo had been slightly painful. It had been hot and humid and by the afternoon a huge thunderstorm had broken over the city. Everest had loomed over us like an invisible weight.

The children of course were oblivious to the magnitude of what lay ahead. They were still in the sweet spot of innocence, glorious naivety. It was one of the attractions of attempting the climb while they were still basking in childhood optimism and hopefulness, to avoid them having to face the reality of the risks ahead.

Marina was quieter than usual. I could sense the weight of Everest on her shoulders. The burden of the unknown that she would carry for the next few weeks as she continued with life back in London while I began my trek deep into the Himalayas. We smiled and laughed, but there was an air of sadness. Perhaps it was the rain and the thunder, but it felt heavy. It clung to us.

And now, here we were at Colombo Airport where our lives would separate. No more family smiles, hugs, laughter …

I waited until the last call for my flight. I wanted to put off the goodbyes for as long as I could.

I scooped up the children who enveloped me like an octopus. I squeezed them and inhaled their smell. I nuzzled their necks and whispered into their ears, 'Look after Mummy.'

'Have fun, Daddy,' they both smiled with that innocence and excitement that only children can muster.

'Please keep safe,' hugged Marina, 'we need you.'

We both cried. I didn't want the children to see my tears. They have seen me cry before and it's important for children to know they can cry, but this felt different. The tears felt like an admission of fear and I didn't want them to fear Everest. I wanted them to be excited and inspired by the mountain.

The tears felt like a weakness, liquid fear. In a way they were. My stomach was knotted and twisted. I have left my family for plenty of risky expeditions over the years, but this one felt different – it felt bigger, taller, badder.

I had struggled to rationalise my yearning to climb Mount Everest with my role as husband and father. After all, being a dad is a primary role. It's not something that you just do part-time. It comes with responsibility and commitment.

I need them and they need me.

Shortly before I left, I had asked the children to give me something special that I could take to the summit with me. Ludo chose his panda teddy bear that he'd had since he was a small child, known as Pandear, and Iona, a little more inexplicably, chose a carrot dog toy.

As well as the two stuffed children's toys, I wanted to take something else. One of Ludo's favourite things in the whole world is his silver shark's tooth necklace. He got it while we were in the Bahamas and he never takes it off. 'Can I borrow your shark's tooth to wear to the summit?' I asked him. It was a big ask, but without hesitation, Ludo placed it around my neck. In its place, I made Ludo a special necklace that I placed around his neck.

That little necklace ceremony was profoundly moving. The silver shark's tooth had such a profound power and energy. It was a reminder always of what was waiting for me at home.

Marina – Saying goodbye

As the dregs of the harsh winter loitered into March, Ben
packed for three months away – two weeks of tropical heat in
Sri Lanka, a teardrop-shaped jewel of a country for an
amazing family vacation, and two months of extreme
altitude in one of the harshest terrains on the planet.

Our holiday was blissful. We travelled through the
verdant land, racing along the endless beaches, surfing and
releasing turtle hatchlings back into the sea. We fell in love
with stray dogs, learned about different curries and watched
in awe as blue whales breached majestically in the
gargantuan ocean. As our halcyon holiday neared an end, I
felt the wave of anxiety welling up in my chest. Our goodbye
was fast approaching, and I wanted to put a pause on our
bliss.

My mother reminded me that I've never been good at
goodbyes as Ben left for the South Pole and my face was a
blurry sea of tears. When my holidays ended and I had to
return to boarding school, my tears would start two days
before I actually left. The anticipation was often worse than
the actual goodbye.

Distraction is the only thing that helps and for me this
came in the form of Ludo and Iona, whose emotions it was
my job to temper.

In the days before we left for Sri Lanka, Ben asked the
children to think of something special for him to take up
Everest. He asked them to give it some thought, and had the

idea that it would be a poignant thing for the film crew to record before he left.

We gathered the children and asked them to fetch the prized objects that Ben would carry to the roof of the world. They disappeared to their rooms and returned shortly after, bearing their prized possessions. With great reverence, they presented to Ben these carefully selected talismans. His eyes looking earnestly into Ben's, Ludo placed a skiing medal (third place) that he had won earlier in the year on a family ski trip. In the meantime, Iona pressed a squeaky carrot dog toy that she had bought in the garden centre that weekend.

A consummate professional in front of the camera, even Ben couldn't hide his surprise. He did a good job at feigning excitement, but he is not an actor and when the cameras had stopped he asked why they'd come up with the choices they had. 'My medal is my most precious thing – it's real gold!' Ludo exclaimed, bursting with pride. 'And I just love my squeaky carrot,' explained Iona. 'I know it's meant to be a dog toy but it makes me laugh, and you know I love carrots!' After a gentle explanation that his ski school medal was not in fact made of a precious metal, Ludo agreed to send his beloved panda with Ben instead: appropriately threadbare and well-loved and conveniently small and light, it fit the bill perfectly. Iona, however, demonstrated all the confidence and stubbornness that we love in our seven-year-old, and nothing would convince her to change her mind.

Ben's flight to Kathmandu left half an hour before our London-bound flight. As his flight was called, he gave the children one last hug, clutching the precious toys they'd

given him to take to the top of the world, Ludo's beloved
shark's tooth necklace around his neck. I gulped back my
tears.

'Make sure you come home safe,' I mumbled through my
sobs as I clutched his broad shoulders and buried my head in
his neck. He nodded and held me tight. 'I love you,' he
whispered, 'don't ever forget that' and with that he was gone,
his tear-stained face turning back to me to wave as he
walked down the long airport corridor.

I hastily wiped the tears off my face, returning to the
children. We sat, perched by the window overlooking the
runway as we watched Ben's plane taxi away, frantically
waving, the children electrified with excitement that we
could actually see his plane and with innocent joy at the
adventure that lay ahead of him; while I tried to muffle my
sobs and crossed my fingers that the luck that had defined
our lives up until this point was not about to run out.

Being a father is my proudest achievement. My children are my
all. I would do everything and anything for them. I would give my
life for them. So why was I risking my life?

Life, of course, is full of compromise. Society installs so many
'values' and 'expectations' on all of us. There is an assumption
when you marry and start a family that you will conform to an
idea of parenthood. And life, of course, is also filled with

sacrifices, but here's the thing: who are you if you have sacrificed the very things that made you the person you were? You are pretending to be the person people *expect* you to be, rather than the person you really are. Isn't that being disingenuous when we as parents are trying to instil confidence and honesty in our children? Are we not being slightly fraudulent ourselves?

When Ludo and Iona were born, I found myself increasingly careful and risk averse. I think it's probably instinct, an evolutionary way of telling us to preserve and protect. The thing about adventure is that it has made me the person I am. Without it, I would be no one. You see, I was never really good at anything. If I'm honest, I am still full of self-doubt. I think psychologists call it 'Imposter Syndrome', the feeling that you are about to be called out any minute.

That time in the Outer Hebrides when I took part in the BBC TV show, *Castaway*, had a seismic impact on my life. I grew. It emboldened me and gave me opportunities I could never have imagined. It gave me the confidence to be who I am. Most importantly it 're-wilded' me. It reconnected me to nature and created an unshakeable relationship with the wilderness. And the wilderness became my mentor.

I am not a religious type, but if I had to choose someone or something to worship then it would be nature. The wilderness possesses the power to heal and nurture, and my year on that windswept island off the west coast of Scotland was like a self-esteem rehab. A detox from the complexities of modern life.

We have such a complex relationship with the wilderness. Man has made it his business to 'tame' the wilderness, but I think it's the wilderness that must tame us.

It's difficult to explain the feeling of freedom and liberty that comes from the wilderness. Of course, there are many different ways we engage with the wild, but for me, the most profound experiences are those in which I have suffered or endured. It isn't the only way to benefit from nature, but it has always given me the biggest returns.

The Scandinavians have a powerful connection with the wilderness; it is written into their language. Where we refer to it as 'nature', they always refer to '*the* nature', which I think adds reverence and power. It shows respect and humility.

I am often asked how I would describe myself. The answer is that I am a modern-day journeyman. The journeyman of old would set out on foot on a travelling apprenticeship. In many ways, that is how I would describe my own life. I am perpetually in motion on an apprenticeship of the wild. There is a spiritual calling to nature. It is profound but sometimes difficult to explain, partly because I have no idea where it will lead.

Mine is a strange life. In many ways, it's that of a 20th-century nomad. I have a family that I love and a beautiful home, and yet I am constantly on the move. I never stop. I rarely have time to settle and dwell, but where does the journey end? Whereas a river empties into a lake or an ocean, I have no idea where my meandering life will lead.

Most jobs or vocations lead to an ultimate goal. Perhaps that of seniority in a company or of financial success or of professional recognition. Mine has no defined or measurable goal.

I am driven and determined, but I have always been guided by instinct and chance. Opportunity has played a big part in my life.

It sounds like a cliché, but I have always lived to seize the moment. I am a 'yes' man.

It is this combination of travel and curiosity with adventure that has been my medicine.

What is adventure? How do you define it? For me, adventure is anything out of the ordinary. It is a break from normality. It is anything that tests you and takes you out of your comfort zone. While it is often synonymous with physical challenge, I think the description is more nuanced.

My own definition of adventure has changed over the years. A little like spicy food: the more of it you eat, the more spicy you want it. Over time your taste buds are desensitised, and you need ever stronger spice.

They also say that your taste buds change every seven years or so, which sounds about right. I used to hate seafood and curry and now they make up the substance of my diet. Fatherhood has unquestionably had an impact: my whole attitude to life has also changed. I find myself looking at life and the world with a new perspective. On one hand, it's with a little more care and diligence in the knowledge that my children will have to live on this planet for the next hundred years or so, but also there is a renewed sense of wonder.

One of the problems of travelling so prolifically is that it essentially devalues the power of my experiences. The impact is lessened through their frequency.

The first big journey I ever took, was when I was 18. I had just finished my A levels and I set out for South America with nothing but a rucksack, a *Lonely Planet* guidebook and plenty of young hope.

I landed in Brazil and spent the next 12 months travelling this exciting new world, experiencing the richness of the food, the people, the cultures and the landscapes. I can still remember that spark of excitement that came with each border crossing and every new stamp in my passport.

That year in South America was a game changer. I came home a different person. I had left a little of me in Latin America. In the interim, I had somehow managed to secure a place at the University of Central England in Birmingham to read Politics. I lived in a little windowless room below Spaghetti Junction and spent my days in the travel section of the city's Waterstones bookshop, leafing through travel guides and travel books.

Two months later, I quit university and set off for Mexico on a one-way ticket.

To be honest, I had no real plans to ever come home. Apart from my family, I had no reason to. I had flunked my exams, left my studies and was working as a barman. I was still living at home and I didn't even have a girlfriend.

Latin America represented excitement, hope and adventure. It was like a shiny beacon at the end of a very dark tunnel.

Travel and adventure have always had the power to heal and transform. The more you put in, the more you get out. The return to Latin America reminded me that the thrill, excitement and challenges of the new and the unknown were intoxicating. It was like looking at the world through a magnifying glass. Everything seemed amplified: sounds, smells, colours. It made my own culture look monotone and bland. Here, everything felt richer, and so did I. I had found work on a turtle conservation project on the Mosquito Coast between Nicaragua and Honduras. I was earning enough to get by, and I had become fluent in Spanish. I had friends. It excited me and it made me feel alive. I was so happy there.

The emotional wealth that comes from travel cannot be under-estimated. Each time I returned from somewhere new, I felt like I had been given a booster. But, of course, everything comes at a cost and I couldn't backpack forever.

When I returned to reality and the comparative mundanity of life, the come-down was immense. When I think back now, I wonder why I ever came back at all. Apart from my family, I had nothing. A couple of terrible A level results and, well, that was it.

I suppose it was the expectations of society in general that drew me home. After all, I couldn't just 'bum around' forever. My parents were heroically silent. They have always allowed me and my sisters to make our own decisions carefully and quietly, help-ing us navigate through the complexities of life.

In their shoes, I think I might have been a little disappointed in me. Both Mum and Dad came from hard-working blue-collar families: my late paternal grandfather was a florist and my late maternal grandfather was an estate agent in Brighton. Mum, the actress Julia Foster, and Dad, the vet, Bruce Fogle, both worked incredibly hard to pay for my school fees.

Underachieving and dyslexic from an early age, I was not a good student. My parents decided to send me to private school to improve my academic levels. Alas, it didn't work so well. But Mum and Dad never said anything. They let me do my own thing.

At the time, the 'right thing' seemed to be to return to Britain and try to get a degree, a job, a career, and a mortgage. I don't want to give the ending away, but it all turned out quite well. That being said, if I were to go back in time, I think I would tell my 19-year-old self to stay where I was.

I love my parents. I love my family and I love my country, but in hindsight there was so much more opportunity overseas. Back home, I was a tiny fish in a pond with 66 million other fish, all hungry for food and space.

But that was nearly 25 years ago. A lot can happen in a quarter of a century. And now, here I was on an airplane heading to Kathmandu for the journey of a lifetime. I was leaving my own family behind, as I set off once again on a journey to a faraway land.

As the plane pulled away from its stand, I could make out two little silhouettes in the window, waving frantically. I sat back in my seat, tears streaming down my cheeks, as I watched the shadows of my two children disappear.

Marina – Am I worried? Not yet

Having dreaded the moment when Ben left us for Everest for months, the reality was not so bad. I was launched back into the chaos of home life, of work, getting the kids to school, of teaching and recording my podcast. Because I had to keep it together for the kids, I ended up having no time to dwell on worry. I had the odd snatched conversation with Ben, but since neither of us are great on the phone, he sent pictures of his trek to Base Camp instead.

A few months before he left, he asked me what I thought of asking my father to join him on the walk to Base Camp.

My father has always loved walking and adventure. It was he who took us as children, often moaning and unwilling, up the Austrian mountains during our long summer holidays. His walking boots were well worn in and he was never happier than when he had my grandfather's old canvas rucksack slung over his back and a pair of binoculars in hand. While resting, his nose was often buried in a book recounting some extraordinary adventure. It was he who first introduced me to the genre of literature that I would become fascinated by, handing me his well-thumbed copy of Into Thin Air *by Jon Krakauer.*

Ordinarily, taking a long period of holiday would have been impossible. For nearly 50 years, my father has been a GP and taking that much time off from his practice would not have worked. However, he'd made plans to retire in February and the March departure of Ben, Kenton and Victoria could not have been better timed.

My father needed little persuading. As a family, our greatest worry was that our father, who seemed to thrive on a busy and full life, would be bored in retirement. He was honoured to be asked, but wanted to check that Ben was only asking him because he genuinely wanted him along, rather than because he felt duty bound to do the right thing.

Having a 70-year-old retired GP on a trek to Everest is probably not something Kenton and Victoria had anticipated. But for years his patients had joked that he'd somehow found the secret to eternal youth, regularly drinking from some fabled elixir that prevented him from ageing. In spite of his years, he is lean and fit and his dark hair is only just starting to become peppered with grey. We were having lunch shortly before he left, after visiting an outdoor shop to kit him up, and I'm sure many people presumed that I was actually his wife.

I loved Ben for asking my father to join him on the walk to Base Camp. I hadn't ever thought about the possibility, but the suggestion was perfect. It shows what a thoughtful and insightful person my husband is. Instead of being consumed by the stress of the preparation of such a mammoth expedition, he continued to think about our families, not blinded by what lay ahead.

The weeks before they set off, I saw the eager anticipation in my father's eyes. 'Well, actually I'm off to Everest,' he'd tell people who asked what his retirement plans consisted of, his eyes twinkling with the thrill of it all. His friends, family, patients and colleagues were beside themselves with excitement. One weekend, as the children played in the garden, I set up an Instagram account so that he could keep us all abreast of his adventures. Within a week, hundreds of friends were following, desperate to follow his adventure.

It was these updates, starting with a selfie of Ben and my father, shortly after arriving in Kathmandu, with flower garlands around their necks, smiling goofily at the camera, that were the highlights of those early weeks. As their trip started, @TheWanderingGP, my father's Instagram moniker, recounted his hair-raising flight into Lukla, the world's most dangerous airport, where the carcasses of less fortunate planes littered the apron and hillside around; their overnights in teahouses and the people whom they encountered on the trail. My favourite showed my father with his arms around Kenton and a Nepali climber, Kami Rita Sherpa, who had summited Everest an astonishing 22 times.

'Between the three of us there have been 33 successful summits of Everest (Kenton 12, Kami Rita Sherpa 21, The Wandering GP 0 (for now)),' he wrote, brilliantly signing off JH (Jonathan Hunt), reminding us that his understanding of the 21st-century phenomenon that is social media would only go so far.

Everywhere I went, all anyone wanted to talk about was Everest, about Ben and how my father was getting on. And inevitably they asked whether I was worried, whether I was sleeping and how I was coping, and honestly, I responded that I was okay ... for now. The reality was that I was only okay because they weren't yet doing the dangerous bit.

CHAPTER FOUR

BAGGAGE

I would describe Kathmandu airport as organised chaos. We navigated around huge piles of grain sacks and boxes being loaded onto the aptly named 'Yeti' Airlines plane. Bags and passengers were weighed. Vast piles of identical, tough North Face kit bags soared like a mini mountain range. It seemed every hiker, trekker, traveller and mountaineer had packed the equipment. And it also seemed impossible that each bag would arrive at the correct destination.

Not that it would be a problem for me, because I didn't have any bags.

Ahead of our expedition, I had spent the best part of six months assembling the best kit and equipment I could. It began when Victoria and I had visited the Manchester factory of PHD, a company that has been making cold-weather expedition gear for years – and which I first came across when I walked across Antarctica to the South Pole. PHD provided a pair of their thick down mitts, which were the best kit on that whole trip, and I had vowed that if ever I was to return to a polar region or to high altitude, I would use their bespoke services.

Victoria and I had caught the train up from London and together crossed the city that had been the home of British Cycling and therefore also her home for many years. PHD still occupies one of the old mills that dominated this part of Northern England. On the factory floor, half a dozen women, who all seemed to be called Margaret, worked on sewing machines, making individual bespoke sleeping bags, jackets and the all-important 'summit suits'.

Jacob, the manager, showed us around the small factory and took us into the 'down' room. It was only after I watched Victoria squirm when she was offered a handful of down feathers that I remembered she is vegan. Despite her animal welfare sentiments, Victoria had agreed, on the advice of high-altitude experts, to use down rather than synthetic filling.

While synthetic filling is a perfectly good substitute in normal life, up in the death zone (anywhere above 7,600 metres) temperatures regularly plunge below minus 40 °C, and a good quality down-filled jacket can mean the difference between life and death.

Victoria had consistently struggled with the cold during our training climbs and we knew that she needed the best insulation in both her sleeping bag and her clothing. We decided to opt for full-down summit suits and sleeping bags which we would then complement with a range of kit and equipment that could be worn underneath.

Before Marina, the children and I set off for our holiday in Sri Lanka, I filled two giant duffle kit bags with all my gear including climbing boots, crampons, harness, ice axe, jumar, summit boots, climbing helmet, summit gloves, pee bottle – everything you need to climb Everest.

I filled a third bag with enough food, treats and snacks to last me the eight weeks on the mountain. One of the side effects of altitude is a loss of appetite. Without food, climbers quickly lose weight, muscle and energy. I knew I had to pack as many things to pique my appetite as possible or risk failure in our summit bid. So, I packed fresh coffee and chocolates, Jelly Babies and kimchee to add to our food. I also bought tins of sardines and packets of salami just in case.

The bags were all carefully packed, labelled and shipped to Nepal weeks before I was due to arrive.

Only they hadn't arrived. Or if they had, no one was sure where they were. I was stuck in Kathmandu, about to climb the tallest mountain on earth, with just the clothes on my back – which amounted to a thin shirt, shorts, a thin jacket and a pair of sandals. To be absolutely honest, I also had a tiny carry-on bag that contained a spare pair of shorts, and my walking boots which I always take in my hand luggage just in case, but that was it.

To make matters worse, we were on a tight timeframe. Most of the climbers had arrived at the beginning of April to give them enough time to walk to Base Camp and acclimatise before their summit acclimatisation climbs – or rotations as they are known.

It was 13 April and we had to be at Base Camp by 20 April if we stood any chance of getting to the summit. Climbing on Everest is only possible in a window of relative calm, just before the monsoon season arrives and with it hurricane-force winds on the summit. This means most attempts happen from mid to late May every year. We had left little margin for error and certainly no time to hang around in Kathmandu waiting for my missing bags to turn up.

We had one day to track the bags before leaving for Lukla on 14 April. They were tracked to customs. It was Friday, a national holiday and the offices would be closed until the following Monday. We had no time to wait. I took a gamble that my bags would catch me up somewhere along the trail.

There is something rather liberating about turning up at the airport with nothing. So often in my job, I travel with a crew and dozens of boxes and bags of equipment. This flight was no different; between Kenton and Victoria there were nearly 20 bags.

This count had been substantially increased by the addition of a new member to our team. I had briefly asked a couple of broadcasters whether they might be interested in our expedition and the lukewarm response had cemented my resolve to climb the mountain without a film crew.

I have a love–hate relationship with the camera. On the one hand, it is my profession, it is essential to my livelihood and it's my day-to-day workmate, but on the other hand it also has the power to dominate. Let's be clear, I owe my entire career to the camera. It is the TV lens that has opened the world to me, but I suppose, like anything in life, it can become a little overwhelming. The camera can be empowering, but it can also do the reverse. At times, I find it has the power to soak up everything in its lens. Great for the viewer, but not so great for the subject.

This happens in a number of ways. Sometimes people reserve and conserve all their energy for the camera – they literally switch themselves on and off – which can be deeply confusing for the people they're working with.

The camera can also become the unintentional 'leader', particularly where a team is involved. People still seem to have a slightly unhealthy reverence for the film camera. I see it all the time. They get star-struck and go all strange whenever a TV crew is about.

When we filmed *Castaway* for the BBC, it was decided that to ensure a more honest, real film, we would film most of the year ourselves. The act of observing will always affect those that are being observed. It is a well-documented truth of psychology, which is why I'd argue that much of modern 'reality' TV is no longer real. It is inhabited by a cast of subjects who are painfully aware of the cameras, often modifying their behaviour for the lens. They simply become caricatures of themselves while they play up for the cameras.

So, after nearly 20 years in front of the camera, I was looking for a break from its prying lens. I saw Everest as a very personal goal and ambition and one I was happy to undertake without the interruption of a camera, because one of the strange side effects of working in front of the lens for so many years is that any type of camera always feels like work, even a stills camera. I know it sounds daft, but I find myself almost allergic to any kind of camera when I'm not working.

But about two weeks before we were due to depart, I had an email from CNN. They knew about our climb and wanted to know if we would make a film. I am very easily swayed, and besides, I thought, it would be a beautiful record of our climb for my children and grandchildren. Agreeing to make a film of the expedition is one thing; making it happen is another. Above all, we had to find a cameraman who was capable of climbing Everest at such short notice. There were only two candidates.

The first was Ed Wardle, a brilliant Scottish cameraman who has climbed Everest with a camera multiple times as well as making his own Channel 4 TV series, *Alone in the Wild*, in which he had spent 12 weeks alone, foraging in the Yukon. Most recently, he had filmed a re-creation of Sir Ernest Shackleton's open boat journey with the explorer Tim Jarvis. In short, Ed was hard as nails and easily up to the task.

The other candidate was more of a wild card. Mark Fisher, a former mountaineering guide from the USA, had filmed with Kenton Cool on a number of climbs. Although he had never climbed Everest, he had filmed at over 8,000 metres and Kenton was sure he was up for the job.

I sent e-mails to both. Ed was busy, but Mark was available and within days he had been signed up as our fourth teammate. Looking back, it was quite a big gamble. I had never met him before. I had no idea what he was like as a person. I didn't know his filming style. Nothing. It was all based on trusting Kenton's references.

A few weeks later, here we were at the airport, with all of Mark's equipment adding height and bulk to Victoria and Kenton's luggage mountain. Slowly, we moved through the bustling airport and soon we were on a little transfer bus that ferried us across the airfield, past the wreck of the recently crashed US-Bangla plane, to our own small airplane.

Flying in the Nepalese Himalayas is not for the faint-hearted. When I'd been out here in January, I'd found myself sitting on the flight out from the UK next to a team of air accident investigators that was on its way to investigate a recent crash on this exact route.

'We come out half a dozen times a year,' one of them smiled.

The first time I flew in the Nepalese mountains was in 2002. I was on Yeti Air and it was without doubt one of the scariest flights of my life.

I was in Nepal with the World Wildlife Fund to cover their work down in Chitwan and Bardia national parks where they were relocating Asian rhino from one park to the other. It was a beautiful experience and while we were out there we flew to the mountains for a couple of days.

I can still remember sitting in the ancient Yeti Airlines plane wondering how safe it was. The windows were tinted yellow and the overall feeling was that I was sitting in a very old airplane. We flew into a massive storm with thunder and lightning. The plane was thrown from side to side, up and down. It lurched, my heart raced and lightning illuminated those yellow windows. I have never been so grateful to land. It remains one of the scariest flights I have ever been on and is the reason I started crossing my fingers on take-off and landing, something I still do to this day.

As testimony to the dangers of Himalayan air travel, it was only a few years later that the WWF team I had been travelling with were all tragically killed when their helicopter crashed in the same area. It still haunts me to this day.

Now, here I was again, 16 years later, making my way to a little plane that would take us to Lukla, which is often described as the most dangerous airport in the world. The reasons for the description aren't hard to work out: it is built into the side of a mountain with a very short runway at the end of which is a very large brick wall. Like I said, flying to the Himalayas is not for the faint of heart.

We all boarded the flight. I crossed my fingers and we began the short journey to the beginning of the biggest challenge of my life.

We flew past soaring white peaks that seemed to tower over the landscape. 'How high is that one?' I asked Kenton, pointing to a mountain that was bigger than anything I had ever seen in my life.

'About 7,000 metres,' he replied.

'And that one?'

'That's 7,200 metres.'

My stomach lurched. These were tiny by comparison. Everest had another mile on some of these peaks. How were we going to do it?

Lukla airport loomed into view on the far mountain. There was no need to descend, the plane would literally fly at the same altitude straight into, or more hopefully, onto the mountain.

We skimmed over a high gorge below. I swear the trees at the summit must have been less than 50 feet from the belly of the plane. My stomach lurched again and a bead of sweat formed on my brow.

Seated at the back of the plane, I had a clear view directly up the aisle and through the pilot's window. It was like being in a simulator, only this was for real, and that near-horizontal, tiny runway directly ahead was our only landing strip.

The mountain raced towards us, or more accurately, we raced towards the mountain, and the pilot slammed our little plane on the runway with such force that I felt sure the landing gear would collapse or the tyres would burst.

There was a loud roar of engines as the pilot threw on the brakes as the plane careered up the runway towards the wall. Then suddenly, silence.

We had made it. There was applause and relief as we descended the steps into the cool Himalayan air.

To speed up our expedition, Kenton had made the decision to bypass the first two days' trekking, because he felt it wouldn't be particularly beneficial to our acclimatisation. Instead, we would take a short helicopter journey to Namche Bazaar, the home of the Sherpa.

When I say short, I mean ridiculously short. It took less than five minutes to soar across the valleys and onto the small helicopter landing pad.

We stepped off from the chopper. The next time we would go high into the sky would be on our own two legs. It seemed incredible that we would be venturing to an altitude so high that helicopters cannot fly there – and the same height that commercial airlines fly.

Namche Bazaar is a tourist hub. This whole region of Nepal is built on trekking, mountaineering and tourism, and the small town is built around the visitors with dozens of small shops selling outdoor clothes and restaurants catering to Western taste buds. We were staying in a little hotel on the outskirts of town adjacent to the Sherpa Culture Museum and the location for Hillary's 1953 expedition.

In the late afternoon, I decided to explore the town a little. I descended the steep steps past dozens of breathless tourists, all bent double over their walking sticks. They were all dressed in trekking trousers with big boots and woolly hats. I must have looked odd in my white shorts and linen shirt that I had worn since leaving Sri Lanka. Luckily, my blood is pretty warm and I hadn't yet felt the need for many more clothes.

I found a little café and ordered a coffee and a brownie. I started having flashbacks, to 2009 when I crossed Antarctica, where we had a mantra that 'eating is training'. The idea was to bulk up to try and counteract the massive weight loss that would come with the effort of walking 1,000 kilometres to the South Pole.

'This is all very civilised,' I thought, as I sat back in my chair and shovelled homemade brownie into my mouth.

'Everest has claimed hundreds of lives …' boomed the solemn voice over on the large TV screen at the back of the café.

'Most of those bodies still litter the mountain,' it continued.

They were showing an afternoon special of one of the many documentaries about Everest. I wanted to stick my fingers in my ears and burble manically to avoid listening.

Don't get me wrong, I *love* these documentaries. I must have watched most of them. I've read all the books and seen all the films, but ever since I'd decided to climb the mountain myself, I'd chosen, rather reasonably, I think you'll agree, to abstain from the mawkishness of them.

But here I was in a café in the Himalayas, my eyes and ears drawn to the film like a moth to a light. I knew I shouldn't, but I couldn't help myself. I found myself watching it with an intensity that I hadn't done before. I found myself analysing each footstep. What were they wearing? What were they eating? It felt a little like sneakily watching a competitor practising before a sports match or event.

Two hours later, I emerged onto the street, my eyes on stalks. It had been a slightly untimely reminder of the dangers ahead. Breathlessly, I worked my way back up the steep steps towards our hotel. Along the way I passed several sherpas, wheezing and coughing uncontrollably. My heart skipped a beat and I wondered, not for the last time, if I had made a huge mistake.

Early the next day, I watched while the rest of the team packed their bags. Still wearing the same shorts, shirt and underwear, I set off clutching just a water bottle and my hat.

There was something rather unremarkable about the first steps on our way to Everest. Back in the 1950s, this would have been an unbelievable task. The route to Base Camp is now one of the most popular treks in the world and before long the route was awash with trekkers of every shape, size and ability and from almost every nation imaginable.

It seems a far cry from the romance and mysticism of those early expeditions when the pioneering mountaineers would have needed to carve out routes between the tiny isolated mountain hamlets. Nowadays, it's estimated that more than 100,000 people descend onto this route every year, and today it felt like they had all come at once.

I had decided to send my father-in-law ahead of us with Sherpa Deepan. I was still worried about how Jonathan would cope with the ever-increasing altitude and the distances we had to cover.

As soon as we hit the trail, Mark, like a mountain goat, kept racing ahead to set the camera up on a tripod, in order to capture some epic walking shots. Naturally, it began to slow us down and it wasn't long before Kenton's smile turned to a frown.

'We can't do this on the mountain,' he harrumphed, 'we need to keep a consistent speed. We can't keep stopping and starting like this.'

It was the first awkward conversation we'd had and was a reminder of the complexities of sharing any journey with a camera. Expedition film-making is very different, especially with a mountain like Everest. The key is not to let the film-making get in the way of the expedition. And now here we were, in the middle of the Himalayas, and Mark was already annoying Kenton. At least it's not me, I thought, as we carried on along the trail.

Nepal is a deeply spiritual place and all along the trail there were little prayer walls, temples, bells and flags. I found myself hypnotically drawn to the multi-coloured, sun-bleached flags as they fluttered in the stiff mountain breeze. Victoria and I found ourselves visiting each and every one of them. It seems a little strange now, but for some reason we felt spiritually compelled. It was like an unstoppable force was drawing us in towards these monuments.

The rough path trailed around the steep mountain that rose on our left; on the right, the valley dropped away dramatically into a deep ravine at the bottom of which we could see the white water of a river as it cascaded over boulders and rocks.

As we rounded another bend of the trail, my eyes were rooted to the path underfoot. I didn't want to trip on one of the roots or rocks. A twisted ankle at this stage would almost certainly end any summit hopes.

'Look up,' smiled Kenton.

My eyes lifted to the horizon and the unmistakable snowy outline of Everest.

Everest. The mountain of my childhood dreams. A mountain that has haunted me my whole life. A mountain I have seen hundreds of times in photographs and films but never in real life. As a child, I used to imagine you would be able to see the tallest mountain on earth from almost everywhere. I soon discovered this was not the case, but I felt sure it would at least dominate Nepal.

The incredible thing about Everest was that this was the first and last time I would see her until our final summit bid from Camp 4 in two months' time.

How can a mountain that is so unspeakably tall, remain so hidden? It still doesn't make sense. But then that is the beauty of mountains. Nothing makes sense. They break all the rules and defy reality.

The sky was clear and the sun reflected off her snowy peaks. A stiff wind whipped snow into curling tongues along her flanks. She looked angry. I stared at her, so familiar and yet so alien. It would be the start of a journey of contradictions.

My eyes scoured her slopes in the far distance. She looked like she was hundreds of kilometres away. To be honest, I was struggling with the notion of reaching her base let alone her summit.

Crowds of trekkers along the route had stopped to take photographs of the distant mountain. I wondered how many of those around me were going higher. In a way, it was the beginning of the psychological battle.

Mountains really are in the mind. As the great Sir Edmund Hillary once said, 'It is not the mountains that we conquer but ourselves.' How true that is. It's like a constant battle of will over sense.

Looking at that mighty mountain, I was overwhelmed with the magnitude of what lay ahead. It probably didn't help that it was only Day 1, we'd already had an argument over filming and I was still wearing my shorts and shirt from Sri Lanka.

I suddenly felt a chill. Both physical and metaphorical. 'Can I borrow a fleece?' I asked Mark. 'Sure thing,' he said, handing me a top. I felt well and truly out of my depth, but there was no stopping us now. Onwards and upwards.

CHAPTER FIVE

LOSS

For six long hours we trekked along the trail to Everest Base Camp. Apart from a few short climbs, it was pretty simple.

It was the start of what would become pretty repetitive over the following week, as we worked our way up the Khumbu Valley towards Base Camp. As we marched onwards towards Pangboche at 4,100 metres, we passed dozens of stupas, Buddhist shrines and places of meditation, and mani prayer wheels. We would meticulously rotate each one clockwise for good karma.

One of the more unusual aspects of life in the public eye is being recognised out of context. In Britain, I have grown used to the notion that if I pop out to the corner shop, more often than not, I will stop to share a selfie or scribble a signature. At home, I anticipate it, plan for it and accept it. But in this internet ready world, where connectivity has no borders or barriers, TV shows tend to travel a little more than they used to. And this leads to some surprising encounters – like being stopped on the streets of

Ulan Bator by a Mongolian who thanks me for my shows and asks for a selfie. Now that is what I call recognition out of context. Let's be honest, I'm not a global A-list superstar, so it still surprises me when I am in a foreign land and this happens.

It seems that here in Nepal, my shows themselves are yet to hit the TV screens, but among the multinational trekkers and hikers along the trail, word had spread that Victoria and I were there.

To be fair, the 'word had spread' was slightly self-induced, by the use of social media.

Like most of us, I love social media and I hate it. I love it for its instantaneous connectivity. It is the first place I search for news, often erroneously, and therein lies the reason I hate it. It has the power to manipulate and exaggerate. But it also has the power to take an expedition like ours straight into people's palms.

Ahead of Everest, in order to enhance the profile of the expedition and to create a way for people to follow our progress, I decided to use Instagram as a medium for sharing the journey. It was a simple way, even with our limited data, to post a picture each day with a small caption explaining what had happened.

Naturally, many others on the route to Base Camp, and in some cases beyond, were following our progress and it meant 'mountain fame'. If I'm honest, I loved it. I have never been someone to 'need' fame; it's not the oxygen of my existence. That's not to say I don't respect it. Indeed, I credit it for most of the opportunities that have come my way. I'm not sure I would be on my way to summit Everest were it not for the public nature of my work.

At home I just get on with it, but here it felt empowering. It was uplifting. It brought familiarity to an unfamiliar landscape. There was something rather reassuring about people stopping to wish us luck and to take a photo with us along the trail. Since we had left Namche Bazaar, the wave of support had grown. In places, we would pass people across the valley who somehow recognised us from a great distance and they would holler, 'Good luck, Ben and Vic!' It always put a smile on my face.

At one of the stupas, a young girl from Yorkshire was busy tying some prayer flags to a metal bar. 'I've left these for you with a prayer,' she smiled before giving each of us a hug. It was deeply powerful to feel such warmth as the ambient air cooled.

Each evening we would stop in one of the 'teahouse' hotels along the route. Every small village or hamlet had a dozen tearooms all offering much the same: a basic bed in an unheated room with access to 'a loo' (also known as 'a hole in the ground') and a little dining room heated by a yak-dung stove.

They were very basic but also very comfortable. Having spent a lifetime roughing it in jungles, deserts and on the ocean, the small comfortable beds were a nice break from the hard ground of camping.

Still wearing my shorts and shirt, I was beginning to feel the effects of the diurnal change of temperature. Where the daytime temperatures often hovered around 20 °C, at night it plunged to way below zero. Each morning I would wake to find my water bottle frozen.

Before dinner, the trail-weary trekkers would huddle around the stove, warming their frozen fingers before a dinner of Nepalese curry was served. Locally called Dal Bhat, it's a very standard curry from the Indian subcontinent that consists of steamed rice and cooked lentil soup, sometimes served with a little extra chicken.

Every morning we would pack up early and head back out onto the trail. Kenton was always keen to leave early and arrive early, to give our bodies time to acclimatise before the next ascent.

There is a very important Puja (blessing) ceremony for every Everest expedition. It is held at Base Camp on a date decided by a local Lama. In the ceremony, the Lama asks the mountain gods' permission for the climbers to climb, forgiveness for any damage caused by the climbing and for the safety of everyone involved. Due to our slightly later departure from Kathmandu, we would miss the Puja ceremony. The sherpas take it very seriously indeed. So, Kenton had decided to make a slight detour to the monastery in Pangboche where the local Lama, Nawang Pal, had agreed to hold an intimate Puja ceremony for us.

For the first time, my lack of extra clothes became an issue as no one was allowed into the monastery in shorts. Once again I had to call on Mark to borrow a pair of thermal leggings to cover my increasingly chilled legs.

Slowly and quietly, we filed into the monastery. Compared to the brilliantly bright sunshine outside, it was gloomy and cool. My eyes struggled to adapt to the low light. As my eyes adjusted to the gloom, I could make out the dozens of flags and tapestries that hung from the walls and the ceiling. In front was a huge, ornate gold carving.

But it was something in the little cupboard on the right as I entered the room that really caught my eye. At a glance, it looked like a hairy cloth. I peered into the cabinet and was astonished to read a little inscription that simply said, 'Yeti Scalp'. One of the holy men who had joined us looked at me approvingly and repeated, 'Yeti, Yeti'. Of all the things I was expecting to encounter on our way to Base Camp, a Yeti scalp was probably the last thing on the list, particularly in this holiest of holy sites. As a child I was obsessed with the idea of the Yeti, or the Abominable Snowman, and this discovery excited me. Later in the expedition, it also put me in huge danger.

Before I had time to dwell on this astonishing discovery, we were all ushered to the floor before Lama Nawang Pal began the hour-long ceremony. Dressed in his brown robes with a red North Face woolly hat, he sat cross-legged and began to chant, beating a single drum with a long, curved stick.

He held little cards as he intoned at a dizzying speed. I would be unable to read words at anywhere near the rate he was singing them. Very occasionally, he would trip over a word or lose his place on the tiny cards from which he was reading, but somehow he always picked himself up and continued. The stumble was barely perceptible.

I sat there on the cold floor, staring around the room. The ceremony had a tremendous power. I could feel the beat of the drum reverberating inside my body. It was powerfully hypnotic. I found my mind drawn to another place. I could feel myself high on the mountain. I could feel the bite of the wind and the chill of the ice.

A single shaft of light pierced through a small window and illuminated Nawang Pal. It was one of the most astonishing ceremonies I have ever encountered. It was both puzzling and powerful.

At the end of the service, he threw rice, something that would become a common theme in the weeks and months to come. As we walked back into the dazzling sunshine, I felt a wave of optimism. I can't really explain it, but I felt I saw myself looking from the summit of Everest.

Both Victoria and I were becoming increasingly in tune with the spirituality of the mountain. Before we left, we made one final clockwise rotation of the monastery, turning every one of the 100 prayer wheels as we went. In the corner was one giant wheel, more than ten feet high and almost six feet wide, I hauled on a single piece of rope, until it had built up enough momentum to begin spinning. I stared, mesmerised, at the multi-coloured wheel chiming the small hidden bells as it turned.

From Pangboche we began the increasingly steep ascent upwards towards Pheriche at 4,370 metres. Once again, Kenton had scheduled an acclimatisation day. But this 'rest' day would be slightly different. In order to speed up our acclimatisation, Kenton wanted to climb to the top of the peak that towers above the small sleepy settlement. At 5,000 metres, it would be the first real test of our expedition.

The four-hour climb was not technical, but it was certainly a good test for our lungs which were still struggling to adjust to the increasingly thin air. Against a backdrop of vast snowy peaks, we scrambled up through the rocky terrain until we reached the first snow. Onwards we trudged until we finally reached the flag-strewn summit.

There was something about those flags, crusted with snow and ice, sun bleached and wind damaged, their vibrant colours in contrast to the browns and whites of the landscape all around. I'm not sure why I found them so profoundly moving, but I did.

Perhaps it was the manifestation of other people's dreams? Others who have made it here, to leave a prayer flag perhaps in memory of someone they have lost, or perhaps in the pursuit of their own dream.

It didn't take us long to descend to Pheriche. From there, it was a relatively short trek to Louche, but before we reached the tiny settlement, we passed perhaps the most poignant place on the mountain: the memorial to those who have perished.

High on top of Thukla Pass is a windswept valley. It is as beautiful as it is bleak. Scattered across the valley ridge are dozens, perhaps hundreds of memorials to those who have lost their lives on Everest. The backdrop of the mountains made clear the reason for the 287 tragedies that have happened on the mountain since the first true mountaineering expedition in 1922.

I was completely overwhelmed, not just by the sheer number of memorials, but by the poignancy of the place. Some of the memorials were little more than a small pile of stones, others were vast stone cairns, while others were simple carved wooden posts in the ground.

The wind ripped across the plateau, freezing our exposed skin. I wandered slowly from memorial to memorial. Occasionally, I would see a name I recognised from the many books I have read about Everest: Scott Fischer, Rob Hall, to name but two.

The tributes stretched across the plateau as far as the eye could see. Each of them was strewn with flags that had been left by loved ones or sherpas who had made the journey to tend to the memorials.

It was profoundly moving to walk among the dead. All of these brave, hopeful souls had come here with the same dream. All there is to remember them by is a small pile of rocks on a wind-swept mountainside.

It felt like walking in a church. I felt deeply respectful of this strange place. There can be few memorial sites in the world as affecting as this one high in the Himalayas.

I sat down next to one of the cairns and stared at the Nepalese writing that marked a sherpa who had lost his life on the mountain. This one, in particular, seemed especially unfair. The sherpas, after all, would probably not be on Everest were it not for the steady stream of dreamers and hopefuls like myself that were drawn to the romance of summiting the world's highest mountain.

I thought about the families who had mourned those close to them. The families that had waved goodbye to their loved ones, just as I had mine. Each and every one of these memorials had a powerful story to tell, some of them well documented in print and even in Hollywood films, others lost forever to the mountain.

Victoria and I sat next to one of the memorials with Kenton who had tears in his eyes as he recalled some of his friends. 'That one is Mark Fischer's,' he said.

'Dude, not cool,' replied our Mark (Fisher) from behind the camera.

'I mean Scott Fischer. *Scott* Fischer,' Kenton repeated.

It was a Freudian slip that hit a little too close to home.

The wind had picked up and was beating across the plateau, snapping at the prayer flags and stinging our faces. I wanted to explore each and every memorial. I wondered how many may never have been visited by friends and family – after all, this wasn't an easy place to get to. Mixed among the handmade cairns were huge boulders, many of which looked like gravestones themselves. Some of the memorials had ornate metal carvings and were adorned with beads and offerings, while others were little more than a small pile of rocks.

It was sobering. Not for the first time, a small wave of doubt washed over me.

Why was I doing this? Who's to say I wouldn't join these romantics who had lost their lives in the pursuit of their dreams? What made me any different?

CHAPTER SIX

COLLABORATION

Walking into Base Camp was like stepping into a parallel universe.

At the entrance to the camp is a large monument marking the end of the route for those trekking to Base Camp and the beginning of the expedition for those going higher. I walked past dozens of emotional trekkers all hugging one another and taking photographs next to the large boulder strewn with hundreds of prayer flags.

For most of those here, this was the culmination of their ambitions. Reaching Base Camp was their ultimate goal. I realised what a huge thing this was for so many people, to reach this remote, once lonely spot, deep in the Khumbu Valley.

'That was the hardest thing I have ever done,' I overheard one American trekker saying to her friend who was on her hands and knees, almost praying to the monument.

It was surprisingly moving to see the raw emotion from those who had made it to Base Camp. There were tears of joy at the culmination of what for many had been a tough 10-day journey through one of the most remote corners of the planet. For us of course, it had simply been a means to an end. We *had* to do the trek to Base Camp to acclimatise, like the bus journey to the start of a marathon.

It was here, at this monument, that our worlds would separate. The Base Camp trekkers would begin their long journey back down the valley towards Lukla, while Base Camp and beyond would become our home for the next couple of months.

A tiny trail led down through a maze of twisting rock and ice into the camp itself. The huge glacier is largely covered in grey and brown rock that gives the impression of a solid valley. The sound of rushing water from the glacial melt had carved a river along the south side of the camp.

Stretching as far as the eye could see were hundreds of multi-coloured tents, all balanced precariously along the rubble-strewn glacier. Yellow and orange dome tents nestled alongside and among dozens of larger tents. Dotted along the mile-long camp were handmade Puja furnaces from which great fans of prayer flags spun out like a spider's web. I marvelled at such an astonishing feat of engineering as I wandered along the main 'path' that transects the camp.

Each expedition team creates their own camp within Base Camp. Sometimes teams are consolidated by larger climbing companies, to share the mountain infrastructure.

The first camp was a team from the Indian Border Patrol. I knew this because they had a large banner across their camp proudly displaying this. Dozens of men in blue tracksuits were busy moving bags and equipment around their sprawling camp.

For 30 minutes we trekked past a spread of mountain-eers from across the world, all of whom would be living here over the next few months in preparation for their summit bids.

We would be 'hosted' by Madison Mountaineering, a company set up by American mountaineering legend Garrett Madison. His company was responsible for hiring the local sherpas, they would source all the food for the expedition and supply the tents. From Base Camp onwards, Garrett and his team would organise the logistics of our operation.

We found our camp halfway up the main site. Twenty orange and white Mountain Hardwear tents were scattered across the site, that included a large blue 'mess' tent and another kitchen tent.

In the centre of our camp, large slabs of rock had been carefully stacked to make a central Puja. It had been draped with a yellow cloth, and from the top of it, a pole had been erected from which fanned out long stretches of prayer flags that radiated out across the whole of Base Camp.

We would be sharing the camp with an assortment of other 'climbers' from across the world. Kenton, Mark, Victoria and I each had our own tent at the far end of our camp, up a little hill of ice which gave us beautiful views over our camp and beyond.

Dominating Base Camp is the infamous Khumbu Icefall, nestled between two huge mountains that guard it like sentries. It 'flows' down the middle of the valley like a river of jagged ice. In the sunlight, it reflects the blue to create the most surreal land-scape. Sometimes it looks like blue lava flowing off the mountain, while at other times it's like a violent ocean that has been whipped into a frenzy of white-capped waves.

In front of the icefall is what is known as the Pinnacles, a large area of jagged ice that protects the entrance. Together, the Pinnacles and the icefall make a formidable gateway to the mountain. Over the coming weeks, I would sometimes sit for hours staring at the icefall, trying to work out how people navigated through the twisted contours and shards of ice. It makes the Wall in *Game of Thrones* look relatively benign.

To be honest, I was very grateful for my own tent. After nearly a week of sharing rooms, it was a relief to get some peace and solitude. More significantly, my bags had made it to Base Camp. They came in on one of the supply-runs by helicopter that regularly touch down at Base Camp. For the first time in 10 days, I could change my underwear.

The heart of the Base Camp was the mess tent where we would have our meals. A communal space, it was where we could escape the intensity of the weather or the claustrophobia of our little tents. In the middle was a table that stretched the length of the tent with camping chairs to seat up to 20. Down the middle of the table was an assortment of herbs, spices, and condiments to help liven up our food.

As I walked in for the first time, I noticed sitting at the table, clutching a steaming mug of tea, the familiar bearded face of former SBS soldier and now TV presenter, Ant Middleton.

I had heard rumours that he was going to be on the mountain and I had contacted him on social media to say hello. It wasn't a surprise to see him here, but I hadn't fully anticipated that we would be living *with* one another in our little camp. Of all the different climbing logistic companies and camps at Base Camp, it did seem incredible that we were both at the same one.

Ant had been sponsored by Berocca and had a Channel 4 TV crew accompanying him. His cameraman was our other candidate, Ed Wardle. Now I knew why he was 'busy' when I emailed him about his availability.

Although I knew of Ant, we had never met before. I had watched a little of *Who Dares Wins*, his SAS series on C4, and had greatly admired his re-creation of the open water HMS *Bounty* journey in which he and his crew spent nearly two months sailing across the South Pacific.

Joining Ant and Ed was Matt, their Assistant Producer (AP) who would be located at Base Camp to help organise gear, charge batteries and be an extra cameraman.

'Couldn't you find a smaller T-shirt?' smiled Kenton a little sarcastically, pointing to Ant's skin-tight top through which his Popeye-esque muscles bulged.

Luckily, Ant has a friendly manner. His presence, although expected, would have an impact on our expedition that I hadn't anticipated. In more than 20 years of film-making, I had never been in such close proximity to another film crew making exactly the same film. Our filming models were almost identical. We were both using single cameraman operators to record our own journeys up Mount Everest. We were sharing the same camp, eating the same food, using the same tents and oxygen up the mountain and even the same sherpas.

The only difference was the people involved. In many ways, it became Ant versus Ben & Victoria. There was no race or winner. After all, both sides had the same objective, we were both facing the same adversity and challenge, but the fact we were both making TV shows added an extra pressure that was unexpected and unhelpful.

I had made a promise to Marina that my full focus would be on the mountain. I wouldn't be distracted by anything else, but the arrival of Ant into the picture created a new testing dynamic. Our film teams had little kit tents next door to one another, and each time something happened in camp, both Mark and Ed were on the scene to document the action.

It was slightly comical. The big difference was that Ant's was a 'secret' climb. He had a social media and news blackout. I was never really sure of his reasons, but I respected his privacy and kept his presence a secret to those following my climb.

We were also sharing our camp with half a dozen other climbers from the USA. Two would-be summiteers had already abandoned Base Camp by the time we arrived. One, a South African, had been here several years before when he was caught up in the tragic avalanche that killed so many. He had returned to exorcise his demons, but just a few paces into the icefall had been enough to overwhelm him with flashbacks, and within the hour a helicopter was speeding him back to Kathmandu.

The rest of our campmates were already heading up the slopes on their first 'rotation', or circuit, onto the mountain. Just as he had done with our two-year preparation plan for Everest, Kenton had a plan for Base Camp.

We would have three days to acclimatise in camp. This would give our bodies a chance to get used to the higher, colder air. It would also allow us to shake off any bugs or lurgies that might be lingering since our trek to Base Camp.

We would then begin a series of rotations onto the mountain, each of increasing height. The first rotation would last for four days and would take us to Camp 1 at 6,000 metres, then on to Camp 2 at 6,500 metres where we would spend a couple of nights before descending to Base Camp.

We would then rest for a couple of days before beginning our second rotation. This time we would bypass Camp 1 and head straight to Camp 2, where we would rest for a few days before heading to Camp 3 at 7,000 metres and then back to Base Camp.

Every team has a different routine and plan, and while many do a third rotation, some only do a single rotation. Kenton explained that the key was to 'touch' Camp 3. We didn't stay there overnight on our second rotation. We literally reached it and then turned around for a return to Camp 2 and then Base Camp.

The rotations require a complex equation of experience and acclimatisation versus exhaustion and wear and tear. In short, the more time you climb the mountain, the more muscle mass you lose and the more exhausted you become.

In the past, some mountaineering disasters have been put down to sheer exhaustion from too many rotations, too high. Some teams rotate all the way to the South Col, or Camp 4, but while this was once the agreed thinking, modern approaches have changed and Kenton certainly stuck to a less is more model.

We needed to hit the targets while maintaining enough energy for the final push to the summit.

Interestingly, Ant and Ed opted for a single rotation before their summit bid. For our expedition, each rotation gave us a chance to get to know each leg of the mountain, from the Cwm to the Khumbu Icefall and the Lhotse Face. The familiarity was settling and reassuring in an otherwise uncertain world. It also allowed us to practise all the climbing skills we would need.

I had always been nervous of using my crampons on sheer ice faces. It requires 'toeing' the blade of the crampon far enough into the ice to take your full weight. That's 80 kilos in my case. It requires absolute confidence and efficiency. Despite plenty of practice over the years, I was still nervous, but the rotations gave me a chance to get into a routine.

It also allowed us to practise using the jumar ascending device with various gloves and mitts. What is easy with bare hands, becomes increasingly difficult as you add layers to your hands. The summit mitts for the higher reaches of the mountain were particularly difficult to use. The temptation was always to remove the glove, but this could be fatal. Bare skin on metal can result in instant frostbite and burn; it also leaves the removed glove vulnerable to falling down the mountain.

One lost glove could be fatal.

We also used the rotations to deposit climbing gear for later on in the expedition. On the first rotation, we took a sleeping bag, mat, snacks, and extra thermals. Then on the second rotation we took summit suits, extra socks, mitts and gloves. We would 'depot' this in a tent at Camp 2, that we hoped wouldn't blow away. Like everything on Everest, it was a gamble, as other teams lost everything when theirs *did* blow away.

Apart from Ant and his team, we had the camp to ourselves. Mark and I decided to explore Base Camp a little. It really is a feat of human engineering, this temporary pop-up city. Home to up to 1,000 climbers, it has yoga studios, a hairdressing salon, an emergency hospital and even a little coffee house among the dozens of camps of varying sizes. Some of them, belonging to the Asian outfitting companies, were home to hundreds including the sherpas.

The sherpas have lived and worked in the mountains for centuries and they have been an integral and vital part of Everest's climbing history. They are the real heroes of the mountain. They work tirelessly, often behind the scenes. They are the silent army that help the hundreds of aspiring mountaineers to the summit each year.

They are the ones responsible for setting up and then dismantling Base Camp each year; our camp alone had taken 20 men a whole week just to flatten out before the tents could all be pitched. They are the ones who help with the cooking and with depositing oxygen on the mountain. They are the ones who carry heavy gear up to Camps 2, 3 and 4. And most importantly, they are the ones who help 'fix', or 'rope' the mountain. It is this 'fixed' rope up the mountain that has attracted so much debate and criticism over the years. It is also, some might argue, the reason there have been so many deaths.

But the fixed rope is the reason relative novices like me can even entertain the dream of climbing Everest. In the past, the attachment of this rope had been an informal, unstructured affair – the collaborative effort of everyone on the mountain. Each mountaineering company had volunteered their finest sherpa to help with the job.

There had been problems in past years with the timings of this fixing which had led to the closure of the whole mountain. This year, however, Garrett, the climbing owner of our hosting company Madison Mountaineering, had taken the responsibility both financially and with the physical resources he had at his disposal to rope the mountain himself. A crack team of sherpas spent days scaling with heavy ropes to help 'fix' the mountain.

It is a sad reality that the number of sherpas on the mountain, and the frequency with which they ascend and descend, means they are also the first to be caught up in tragedy. Many sherpas have perished on Everest, which is also cause for controversy. Critics have pointed out that if it weren't for the wealthy climbers who try to tackle the mountain year upon year, the sherpas wouldn't be put in harm's way. It's the selfishness of climbers, in other words, that causes so much death, these critics argue.

I had asked our team of fresh-faced, keen sherpas what they thought about the criticism and whether they thought it was well founded.

'We are mountain people, we love the mountains,' explained Sherpa Ang Thindu. 'The climbers give us the opportunity to do what we love.'

Nepal is second only to Bangladesh as the poorest country in Asia, with an average family income of about $500 per year. The average sherpa can earn many thousands of dollars each season, while the coveted role of working with the summiting climbers on the final rotation can earn each accompanying sherpa a bonus of thousands of dollars per client. Of course, the most famous sherpa of all, Sherpa Tenzing, was, with Hillary, the first to summit Everest. Tenzing, long since passed, is still a national hero in Nepal.

The dangers are obvious, but no one forces them to do it. There is plenty of low-risk work with the 100,000 trekkers and hikers who walk to Base Camp each year, but the comparative low pay and monotony draws plenty of sherpas higher up the mountain.

There is no doubt there was a period of exploitation when sherpas were underpaid and underinsured for their work, but the watershed came after the avalanche at the icefall in 2014 and the loss of more than a dozen lives.

There was outrage at the tragedy. How had it happened and who would help their grieving families financially? Things have quite rightly changed since then, and sherpas now have access to all the same equipment, food and facilities as the paying climbers, as well as life insurance and primary health care.

I loved being with the sherpas. While they often spent time in our mess tent, they preferred to gather in their own mess tent complete with burning incense and a Puja where they would sit and gossip over herbal teas.

Their tent had a beautiful, spiritual, soothing karma. I used to feel calmer just walking in. There was always a reassuring warmth when you entered. With their constant smiles and their glowing eyes, the Nepalese have a happy way about them. If we Brits are Down, they are defiantly Up. They have a gentleness that is infectious and uplifting.

I used to spend hours just sitting. Being, absorbing. It was like recharging my batteries. Our Base Camp was made up of three worlds: the mountain itself, the mess tent which was the world, and the sherpa tent which was Nepal. I would drift and migrate between the three of them depending on my mood.

The food at Base Camp was pretty incredible. I have no idea how the cook was able to rustle up such amazing fare each day.

From freshly baked bread, pastries and pancakes each morning to fresh fillets of beef and even chips for dinner. The important factor that the mess tent catered for was in the variety of foods on offer. Altitude has the effect of stripping you of your appetite. I was never sure from one minute to the next what I craved or what would make me feel sick. But there was always enough of a variety of options that something would look attractive to eat. The winner was usually the Nepalese classic, Dal Bhat curry, which is white rice, lentil soup and a little chicken.

There is a lot of hanging around in Base Camp, and we would spend much of the day sipping tea and chatting about our lives and our loved ones.

In the weeks that I would spend at Base Camp, we didn't socialise a great deal outside of our camp. There is a collective phobia about germs and illness that dominates the whole site. We became obsessive about disinfecting with hand gels. A lurgy could ruin all hopes before we had even begun. Some camps insist on a sort of quarantine, not allowing anyone in or out. The result is a fear of anyone who sneezes or coughs.

'Make sure you sneeze into your elbow, not onto your hand,' we had been told by Garrett on arrival. 'And if you have to cough, try and go outside; and if you have a bad tummy, try and quarantine yourself until you're better.'

Victoria said it reminded her of the Olympics where athletes are terrified of illness before competition. The fear and anxiety over ill health was overwhelming. A single sneeze or cough was met with suspicious scowls.

Our loo consisted of a large, blue plastic barrel with some wooden steps up to a wooden loo seat on the top. Once filled, the barrel would be sealed and carried down the mountain to be emptied at a sewage treatment plant.

This meant that the barrel could only take solid matter, as any liquid would leak during the journey off the mountain. So ablutions had to be carefully planned. You had to pee into a hole in the snow and ice first and then sit down to do a number 2 afterward. It takes a bit of control over muscles, but it didn't take long to master.

Incredibly, there was even a shower. Another blue plastic barrel was filled with glacial meltwater and was elevated on a hill above a little tent. The gravity-fed pipe was connected to a simple shower head that was connected to a propane burner which heated the water.

You had to plan and book a shower way in advance, and it was only ever advisable in the middle of the day when the sun was high in the sky and the water wasn't frozen, but it was heavenly. I only had two showers the whole time I was there, but both of them were highlights of an otherwise uncomfortable experience.

To wash clothes meant walking to the little glacial meltwater stream and using a non-toxic biodegradable soap. We would wash the dirty clothes in chilly waters, before hanging them on the washing line to dry. The side of the clothes facing the sun would dry instantly, while the opposite side in the shade would almost instantly freeze solid with ice. You would simply rotate the line and let the ice melt before the clothes would dry.

Despite the isolation and remoteness of Base Camp, we had access to pretty good mobile and internet services. It was always weather dependent, highly unreliable and expensive, but when it worked it was incredible.

It meant that I could post updates on my Instagram account and file copy for the various newspapers that were covering our climb. But by far my favourite connection was calling in to my children's school for a live assembly.

I sat on a pile of rocks overlooking the Khumbu Icefall and called in to the school in Notting Hill where three hundred 5–12-year-olds were all sitting cross-legged in the hall. Mr Borthwick, Ludo's head of year, had connected the phone to speakers and my voice reverberated around the room. Among those little children were Ludo and Iona, listening to their Daddy capture the essence of the mountain in a monologue to the children.

'I am living in a little tent on a moving glacier. At night I can hear the groaning, creaking of the ice as it contorts under me, followed by the loud boom of an avalanche as it tumbles off the mountain in a great cloud of rubble and dust. We poo in a bucket and wash our clothes in an icy little stream. We are already at 5,500 metres where the air is thin enough to steal your breath, while all around me are the snowy peaks that soar thousands of metres into the sky. Look up and imagine them disappearing miles into the sky. Well, that is my world. It is a world of whites and greys. There is no colour here, apart from the prayer flags that flutter and flap in the ever-present wind. I have a little tent to myself in which I have my worldly belongings. I have a little mattress and a thick sleeping bag to protect me from the bitter temperatures that freeze my water bottle solid. At night, I pee in a bottle that I then use as a hot water bottle in my sleeping bag. I have some photographs of my family and a big bag of chocolate that I no longer want to eat, as the thought of it makes me sick. Altitude makes you lose your appetite. I never thought I would say no to a Cadbury Twirl.'

I then opened the assembly to questions: 'Is it dangerous?', 'Are there any animals?', 'What will you do when you reach the summit?'

I loved doing that assembly. I could picture Ludo and Iona sitting among all those little children. I had sent them some videos I had made on my iPhone around camp that they played after I ended the phone call.

Part of the draw of the climb was to not only inspire my own children, but all children. I tried to imagine their little faces as I told them about avalanches and peeing in bottles.

A couple of hours later, Marina sent me a short video of 300 screaming children shouting in unison, 'GOOD LUCK, BEN', and at the front were Ludo and Iona, confused as to whether they should say Ben or Daddy. It still makes me cry just thinking about it. I must have watched it a hundred times, I could make out Iona mouthing the word 'Daddy'. It was the most beautiful video I ever received.

Let me tell you something about emotion. Altitude has a very strange effect on it. Have you ever been on an airplane and found yourself weeping at a relatively unemotional film? There is scientific proof that altitude makes people more emotional and, boy, was I suffering on Everest. The smallest thing could set me off. Over the next six weeks, I would be surprised by how easily the smallest of things could set me off crying. Marina had packed me off with 50 envelopes, inside each of which was a photograph. She had got the children to scribble a message on each one. She had packed enough for one per day. I was always torn between happiness at the memory and the sadness of the separation.

I had noticed throughout our two years of climbing together, that Kenton was often emotionally fragile. He would often become teary while recounting stories. I think it was partly the skeletons of loss in his cupboard, of those friends he has lost to mountaineering accidents over the years, but I also now know it is the effect of altitude. Victoria, too, had become more emotional. We all felt the effects.

As comfortable as it was, camping at such altitude still took its toll on the weak, the elderly and the infirm. My father-in-law had astonished all of us with the speed and strength of his trek to Base Camp, but the thin air and the cold were starting to affect him. The altitude had rendered him nauseous and I head-held him as he vomited. Each night I had tucked him into his sleeping bag which I had doubled up with my own high-altitude bag that would eventually come up to Camp 4 with me. Even with two sleeping bags, he was struggling with the freezing night-time temperatures. We had also given him a bottle of oxygen to recharge his weakened body during the night.

Marina had suggested he stay for the duration of the expedition, but just two nights was enough to realise he was ready to leave.

We had spent three days at Base Camp and Kenton had planned that we would begin our first summit rotation onto the mountain the following day. It seemed an appropriate moment for Jonathan to head home. I organised for a helicopter to take him and some sick sherpas back to Kathmandu.

It was surprisingly emotional to say goodbye to Jonathan. Despite knowing him for nearly 12 years, I had got to know a very different side of him. For a start, I got to call him by his real name.

'You know, I'm not actually called Jon,' he had told me after I'd introduced him to some fellow trekkers in a teahouse one day.

I felt slightly embarrassed that it had taken him 12 years to correct me. I had heard his family call him by both names, but had always known him as Jon. During this journey, I had come to know not Jon, but Jonathan. I had felt a great familial instinct to look after him and to make sure he had the best experience possible. As worried as I often was for his health and wellbeing, it was always an overreaction on my part. He had been a picture of health throughout and had kept everyone's spirits up with his endless stories.

Not only had he gone to Charterhouse, the same school as one of the first mountaineers on Everest, George Mallory, but he shared a name with John Hunt, the leader of the famous 1953 expedition that first climbed Everest, who also happened to have lived in the same village as him. Jonathan had become a part of our strange, eclectic team. He had also been an inspiration to all of us. So many people see retirement as the beginning of the end, but he had started his retirement as he wanted to live it: brightly, with ambition and fortitude.

The long trek had overwhelmed hikers half his age, and despite never admitting it, I knew he had pushed through his own limits on occasion. It was his gritty determination that we all found admirable, and his good humour had turned what may well have been a banal hike to Base Camp into part of the adventure.

His presence was a reminder to enjoy every minute of it. One day, I had overheard him chatting with Victoria. 'I'm so glad you're here, Jonathan,' she said. I loved hearing that was how she felt.

My favourite part of the time we spent together was undoubtedly at a cold, dark teahouse in Pheriche. Cramped into a pretty bleak little room after a hard day of climbing, we were all shattered. The steep climb and the added altitude had particularly taken its toll on Jonathan.

I don't think Jonathan will mind me telling you that he isn't very 'techy' so, at first, for his Instagram account, I would get him to dictate what to post, but in the end I took to writing my own 'copy' next to the photographs and posting them on his account.

That evening, when I checked my e-mails, someone had sent through a newspaper headline.

'Ben Fogle's father-in-law sent to "keep an eye" on him and former Olympic cyclist Victoria Pendleton.'

As we all lay together huddled from the chill and trying to capture warmth from the yak-dung burner, I read the article to my father-in-law and the rest of the room.

'Most wives would worry about their husbands disappearing on a nine-week adventure with an alluring Olympic star who boasts model good looks.

'So television explorer Ben Fogle's wife of 12 years, Marina, could be forgiven for taking the precaution of sending her father, retired GP Jonathan Hunt, to accompany them.

'"Marina's not a jealous type, but she wouldn't be human if she didn't have a few doubts about letting Ben go on the trip," one of her friends tells me. "Her dad will be keeping an eye on Ben."'

'You're making it up,' Jonathan chuckled, a broad grin across his face. The room exploded into uproarious laughter. 'Stop it,' he laughed uncontrollably, 'it isn't real, you must be making it up.'

I looked around at us. I was still wearing the same clothes I had been in for nearly 10 days now, including the same underwear that was practically walking (my father-in-law had even offered me a pair of his own pants which I thought very generous and strange at the same time).

Victoria was bundled with about 50 layers of clothes. None of us had washed in more than a week. Jonathan and I were sharing an ice-cold little room with a moth-eaten blanket and our pee bottles on the bedside shelf.

And this was the newspaper headline. It was honestly one of the funniest moments I can remember. To see the joy and happiness in Jonathan's eyes at the ridiculousness of it all, will remain with me for a long time.

A little like our journey, it was surreal and contradictory.

The article then continued: '*Marina's father is the pair's team doctor … He has even created an Instagram account to share photos along the way.*'

At this point, tears streamed down Jonathan's face as he bent double in a fit of giggles. So much had been made by the whole team about his Instagram handle (the one I was doing) and now it was even in a national newspaper. I never thought I'd say it, but 'Thank you, *Daily Mail*' for bringing such joy and laughter to what would otherwise have been a cold, dark night.

Now it was time to say farewell. Apart from saying goodbye, it also felt like cutting my final tie to Marina and my family. Jonathan brought a sense of connection. A comforting familiarity in a hostile new place.

He had become a crutch. I liked having him there. It brought a sense of normality to the chaos of the unknown and the fear of what lay ahead. We hugged and he clambered into the chopper.

'Take care,' he hollered as the helicopter lifted and shot off down the valley. One chapter had ended and another was about to begin. Tomorrow, we would set foot on the mountain for the first time.

Marina – The media

It seemed to be a slow month for news. Having announced his Everest bid, the British media were keen to eke what stories they could from it. Our collective favourite was a piece in a Sunday paper, in which 'a close friend' had divulged that the real reason my father had joined the expedition was 'to keep an eye on Ben and Victoria'. Sitting under an apple tree in my mother's garden on an unseasonably hot Sunday afternoon, my mother, sisters and I laughed until tears streamed down our faces at the hilarity of the idea.

The following week, Ben posted a picture of Victoria and him huddled together in a tent. 'Tent selfie at 6400m with @ victorialou,' he'd written. Underneath, my sister, Olivia, had commented, 'hmmmmmm … and no father-in-law to keep an eye on you guys ...' Cue a call from a journalist desperate for something to write. 'Are you worried?' she asked. 'I mean it looks like Ben and Victoria are getting very close and even your sister seems worried,' her mock concern betraying the desperate hope that she was on to something. 'Considering that Ben hasn't changed his clothes for four weeks,' I retorted, 'rather her than me.'

CHAPTER SEVEN

FEAR

The first time I realised that I was scared of heights was when I was about 10 years old and on a trip to Wales with my friends Ben (everyone was called Ben back then), Barnaby and Toby. (They don't make names like those anymore.)

Ben's family had a little farmhouse in the Brecon Beacons and we decided to climb the mountain behind the house. I say mountain, when it was probably more of a hill, but to a group of primary school kids it was a Himalayan-sized challenge.

The four of us and our odd collection of dogs that included two golden retrievers, two King Charles cavaliers and some cocker spaniels all set off to summit our first Welsh peak.

The dogs scampered ahead, leaping from rock to rock as they ascended the hillside with ease. We squelched through mud and scrambled through little moss-covered waterfalls until we were nearly halfway, when we hit our first obstacle, a large outcrop of rock that was just too high for the smaller ones in the group to clamber over (basically, that meant me).

The others, including the pack of dogs, all scrambled over the rock, but I simply didn't have the height, leg length or the strength to pull myself up. For 10 minutes, I struggled against gravity until I finally hauled myself up on my belly.

Wet and muddy, we continued to scramble up the rocky and ever increasingly steep hillside until we reached another large rock. This one was even bigger. The drop was more sheer. My heart began to race with panic at the realisation that I wasn't going to get up. Worse was the suffocating fear that had swept over me as I realised how far the drop was. I was marooned. In the blink of an eye, I found myself unable to go up or down. I crouched low and cried. My friends looked at me with a mix of panic and amusement as I sat there refusing to move.

I can still remember the overwhelming sensation of fear. I had never experienced it before, but I now know it was the early development of vertigo. I felt a sense of helplessness as I looked down to the valley below. I could quite clearly see the little farm-house with wood smoke coming from the chimney. It was so close and yet so far. The boys descended for help and several hours later I was helped down by Ben's father.

It was my first experience of uncontrollable panic. The first time I had found myself frozen with fear. Unable to move or think. I tried to avoid mountains after that, but the romance and excitement soon drew me back, and nearly a decade later I found myself in Ecuador, South America trying to climb the highest active volcano on earth.

It was my gap year. Technically, it was my first gap year, but let's not get bogged down with technicalities. I was living with an Ecuadorian family in Quito, the capital of the Andean nation. Each day I would look out of my window and see the snow-capped wonder of Cotopaxi. At nearly 6,000 metres, it was considerably higher than the few hundred feet of Welsh hill that traumatised my childhood, but the optimism of youth, or perhaps it was amnesia, attracted me like a moth to a light.

After nearly a year of staring at that mountain glistening in the Andean sun, I found myself romping up its peak with my friends, Guy and Guy (if you weren't called Ben in those days, you were probably called Guy). We found a guide and hired some cold-weather gear, boots and crampons. The shock of climbing from 4,500 metres to the mountain hut at 5,000 metres is what sticks in my mind. It was just 500 metres. I could see the hut. There was a path all the way there. But it was like my rucksack had been filled with bricks. Each step was leaden.

At the refuge, one of the Guys developed acute altitude sickness. His face puffed up and his gums began to bleed. So only Guy H, myself and our guide headed off in the early hours for the summit. All was fine, until daybreak. Beneath me, the drop felt dizzying. I didn't know where to look. I wanted to scrunch my eyes closed and pretend I was somewhere else.

The weather had turned and we found ourselves in our own mini-mountain drama. We summited in zero visibility and ended up getting lost on the descent. After we failed to return to the refuge, a search party was dispatched. It was pretty terrifying and humiliating in equal measure. I decided to hang up my rented climbing boots and axe.

*   *   *

It didn't take long before I was seduced back to the world of mountains. I was studying at the University of Costa Rica where I had been stabbed during a mugging and had decided to head to Bolivia to recover. It was here in La Paz that I decided to try one more mountain. I'm not sure why. I don't know if it was to overcome my fear of heights, or perhaps it was just the unstoppable draw of the mountains?

Whatever the reason, I signed up to scale the 6,000-metre Huayna Potosi, a popular Bolivian climb. Everything went well until I reached base camp. A winter storm had turned the soft snow into an icy slab. It was impossible to get the tent pegs into the ground, so I stupidly left my tent unsecured. At midnight, as we were getting ready to leave for the summit, a gust of wind blew my tent complete with all my gear off the mountain side, leaving me standing on the exposed mountain in my thermals with just a pair of boots. For better or worse, I never had time to ascend and confront my vertigo, as I was too busy scouring the mountain for my missing kit (which I did finally find).

It would be a further decade before I faced another mountain. I was filming for a BBC series called *Extreme Dreams* in which I took groups of people on life-changing journeys and expeditions around the world.

One of the dreams would be to try and summit the 6,300-metre Chimborazo in Ecuador. This was a formidable mountain to attempt. It was considerably higher than anything in my previous experience and would test my vertigo to its limit. What's more, I was effectively the 'team leader', guiding others equally fearful of heights, across the Andes.

The whole thing was pretty terrifying, not that I ever admitted it at the time. I tried to use my professionalism on screen to hide the fear that pumped through my body in a rising bile of pure panic. The higher we climbed, the more exposed we became and the more out of control I felt.

Bad weather had hampered our climb, and low cloud and poor visibility had cloaked the mountain top ahead of our final summit bid. We made it to the last camp, but as we began the final climb towards the summit we were beaten back by the weather and had to return to base camp having failed to summit. We all felt dejected and beaten, and my vertigo had gone largely unchecked. It felt like the mountains were trying to tell me something.

My fear of heights wasn't restricted to mountains. A year after our failed climb, I was in Bristol for the BBC's *Countryfile* to make a film about the International Balloon Fiesta. I had never been in a hot air balloon before and we had been invited to fly with Nick Langley of the Airship and Balloon Company.

We took off in our simple wicker basket and soared above Bristol where we joined hundreds of other balloons. Everything was fine, until our pilot took us a little higher. As I peered over the edge of the basket, I felt an uncontrollable urge to jump out. I had never experienced this feeling before. I felt a wave of panic and my legs buckled under me as I sank further into the basket for security. It was terrifying. I squatted in the corner until our pilot descended.

Being at height is one thing. Leaping from it is a whole other ball game. To this day, the swimming pool where we learned to swim as kids is a powerful memory. It had one of those massive concrete, multi-platform diving boards. While my sisters and other children were happy to leap from the 10-metre board, I could barely make it from the 1-metre. Occasionally, I would test my resolve by walking out to the 5-metre board. I would stand on the edge of the board, my legs shaking, heart pounding, feeling sick to my core. I can remember my sisters goading me to leap. 'Come on, Ben!' they would shout, but the more they shouted, the worse it became. The longer I stood there, the more people built up in the queue behind me. The pressure intensified and the height seemed to grow until it was a vertiginous drop into the unknown.

A few years ago, I made a series for the BBC called *Ben's Year of Adventures* in which I travelled the world in pursuit of fear and adventure. To get things going, I went Coasteering – a sport which has been described as a blend of 'rock-hopping, shore-scrambling, swell-riding, cave-exploring and cliff-jumping' – along the Pembrokeshire coast in Wales. I was filming with my friend and former SBS soldier, Bernie Shrosbree. Shortly before we completed the section of coastline, we reached a 15-metre cliff. Sink or swim, I had to leap off the cliff into the swirling waters.

'You can do this,' I repeated to myself as I walked to the edge of the sea cliff. I looked down and once again was overcome with an uncontrollable fear. I felt sick and dizzy. I turned and walked away. 'Focus,' I berated myself as I walked back to the edge. 'You can do this.' Again I was overcome with vertigo. The more I stared at the water below, the greater the drop appeared to get. Every part of me wanted to give up. I began to panic and the longer I took the worse it became. I hated myself for it. I was failing again. I couldn't do it.

'Come on, Ben,' implored Bernie, 'focus, breathe deep and just jump.'

It took me 45 minutes before I went for it. I walked away from the edge. A few paces away, I turned and ran. It felt like I was falling for minutes. The feelings of euphoria and release were extraordinary. It felt like one tiny leap in overcoming my vertigo.

But it was my solo skydive for the same series that really tested my resolve. We were in Australia in Perth and the idea was that I would have a two-day crash course in skydiving before making the leap myself, on my own – a pretty terrifying prospect, I think you'll agree, for someone so fearful of heights. I couldn't sleep the night before the jump. I lay in my bed imaging the fear of that freefall.

The next day, as the plane circled tightly to gain maximum height, I wondered if I had finally overstretched myself, placing hopeful ambition ahead of sensible thinking. At 12,000 feet, the little aircraft door opened and I felt a rush of cold air as I slid my bottom to the edge. I dangled my legs over the edge and looked down at the tiny world below. It felt like an out-of-body experience. How could I do this?

Once again, it was the fear of humiliation that focused the mind. I had to do this. Professionalism and drive cleared my head as I counted down from 10. An instructor joined me, counting down with his fingers.

Five, four, three, two, one ...

Despite every bone in my body wanting to coil back into the plane, I threw myself into the thin air. 'F**k it,' I thought, as my body tumbled. It's a strange feeling to smother self-preservation with wanton risk and fear.

I plummeted through the air, and soon function and performance took over. The fear drained from my body and those little endorphins flooded through me, like I was in a drunken euphoria.

The feeling was extraordinary, but I was far from purging fear from my body.

My personal fears are far more complex than just vertigo. While few are numbingly overwhelming, I have had to confront a range of fears over the years. I'm not going to digress too much here, but I think it's interesting to try to understand my psyche and what it is that attracts people like myself to confront those fears.

I'm often asked when I have been most fearful, and while I could use examples of being in a capsized boat in the middle of the Atlantic or stuck in a collapsing crevasse field in Antarctica, I think my greatest fear happened in the Okavango Delta of Botswana.

I had been making a film about conservation in Africa with Princes William and Harry. It was a pretty surreal experience and one night I found myself around a campfire sandwiched between the two royals while a fellow conservationist shared extraordinary stories from the African wilderness.

One story stood out. Brad Bestelink is a South African conservationist who had come to Botswana to help run one of the camps with his wife, Andi. Keen scuba divers, they had been desperate to dive in the floodwaters of the Okavango Delta. Two things kept them from pursuing their dreams: crocodiles and hippos. These two animals, between them, are responsible for more human deaths in Africa than any other species.

They decided to recce a stretch of water. For many weeks, they observed the habits of the local wildlife and one day, confident that there were no hippos or crocodiles in the water, they took the brave decision to dive in. With full scuba gear and no protection, they leapt into the unexplored aquatic world. No one had ever braved this underwater world before, for obvious reasons.

They swam around in the 10-metre clear water, euphoric that they had defied the sceptics and survived a swim in the crocodile-infested waters, when suddenly from the depths appeared one of the prehistoric reptiles.

Brad and Andi were pretty sure they were about to become lunch, but remarkably the creature swam off. It appeared that the crocodile had no reference point for 'bubble-making scuba diver', unsure of whether they were friend or foe, predator or prey, so it left them alone.

The two divers emerged from the water, elated and relieved. The next day, they decided to put their theory to the test. Once again, a crocodile appeared but left them unscathed. The very unscientific principle of 'crocodile swimming' was born.

Over the campfire, Brad invited the young Princes and me to join them for a dive. Unsurprisingly William and Harry were 'too busy', but yours truly jumped at the chance and soon the opportunity had morphed into a full scientific expedition. We teamed up with Adam Britton from Australia who is widely recognised as the world's leading expert on crocodiles, and within a few months I found myself back out in the Okavango Delta having swapped a prince for a crocodile.

The aim of the televised expedition was simple. By understanding more about the underwater behaviour of crocodiles, we hoped to reduce the number of attacks on humans in the area. The water of the Okavango Delta is a lifeline for Botswanans who use it to wash, to drink and to clean. Attacks are unnecessarily frequent, and we hoped that by understanding how crocs behave, we could save lives. Simple really.

The essential safety principle behind 'crocodile diving' is to make sure you dive in cool, clear waters and that you maintain a visual on the Nile crocodiles themselves. Dressed in full scuba gear, the team would sit in a fast, rigid inflatable speedboat as it raced along the narrow river system. When we spotted a sunbathing crocodile, we would wait for it to slide into the waters before following it in. The key to a safe dive was to get into the water before the crocodile found a place to hide underwater.

Armed with a metal stick each for protection, we prepared to make a 'rapid entry' into the water – the aquatic version of free-falling. I will never forget the overwhelming feeling of fear the first time I went into the water, with all my senses telling me to stay within the safety of the rubber boat.

Under the burning African sun, I watched as a mighty 7-metre-long killing machine slid effortlessly into the water. As I sat on the side of that boat in full scuba gear, my heart pounding, sweat dripping down my face, I have never and probably never will again experience fear on that scale.

The fear of the unknown. The fear of vulnerability. The fear of the unpredictability. There were so many facets. My mind was torn between a natural sense of self-preservation and trying to believe the theory of those naturalists and behaviourists around me, on whose word I was relying, and on whose word my life depended.

There is a common assumption that it is impossible to die, or even become injured, when there is a camera present. We all experience it. For some reason, the presence of a camera and a cameraman usually means wellbeing and safety and certainty. Television likes jeopardy, but it prefers manufactured jeopardy. Controllable jeopardy. The result is that we have a habit of feeling more secure when a camera is around.

As I have learned on various occasions, this really isn't true. Despite the prying lens in my face, I felt a vulnerability I had never experienced before. I knew it was now or never. The longer I waited, the more dangerous my circumstances.

I held my mask to my face and fell backwards into the water.

The world went from a sharp and cheery brightness to a green and brown aquatic murkiness. It felt like stepping into an alternate reality. What surprised me the most was how chaos and fear instantly turned to focus and awe. I got within a couple of feet of a wild Nile crocodile on that first dive, and I can honestly say it was one of the most exhilarating things I have ever done. Over the course of the following few days, we took dozens of dives, and with each one we became a little more confident and brazen.

Then one day, we lost our focus. Our cameraman, Mike, a veteran of many risky dives, was delayed in his entry to the water. By the time Mike reached the river bed, an enormous Nile crocodile had snuck up behind him. He understandably got a bit of a shock. The crocodile sensed his fear and it went for him. Luckily for Mike, he was armed with a huge camera in a waterproof cylinder. He stuck it into the crocodile's jaws and it soon realised that he wasn't as tasty as a catfish and it swam off into the depths.

It shocked all of us. The hardest part was that we were only halfway through the expedition. Should we quit and go home? We tried to understand what had gone wrong. One of the toughest decisions I have ever had to make was whether to get back in the water or not. What if it happened again?

In the end, we decided to continue. Mike even wrote a 'just-in-case' note for his family. We were defiantly skirting with death on that one, but somehow we got through it unscathed, though the psychological scars remain.

I say psychological scars, but I should probably rephrase that to psychological armour. I learned a lot about fear and its control during that African expedition. I was as far out of my comfort zone as I have ever been.

Until now. Here on Everest.

It was the night before our first rotation onto the mountain. I couldn't sleep. We would be up early to try and climb to Camp 1 before the heat of the day.

CHAPTER EIGHT

RISK

It was 3 am. I hadn't slept a wink. I lay awake as the chilled air froze my beard. Huge avalanches cascaded down the mountains above, and tumbled into the valley with terrifying booms that reverberated through the air. I could feel the powerful bass notes penetrating deep down into my very core. Sometimes it sounded like thunder. At other times, it was like the mountain was roaring. A beast growling, reminding us who was boss.

I had watched countless avalanches during the daytime, but they always sounded so much worse at night, perhaps due to their invisibility. My imagination would run wild. What if it reached my tent? What if it buried us? What if it fell onto the Khumbu Icefall? The icefall loomed large in my thoughts. It dominated my hopes, my dreams; my fears and my nightmares.

For four long days, I had stared at her. Like so much of the landscape, she looked beautifully wretched. I would spend hours watching and wondering. Wondering how anyone could navigate through her broken, cracked, icy bosom. Occasionally, I could make out the tiny silhouettes of climbers as they worked their way through the icy labyrinth. They would appear and disappear as they climbed and ascended the maze-like landscape. Like tiny ants, they looked so vulnerable.

Marina – The icefall

The biggest problem is not the altitude, or the mountain itself, but the fact that the most dangerous part of the whole mountain lies just above Base Camp, meaning that every time they ascended, they'd have to negotiate the notorious Khumbu Icefall. Essentially a frozen waterfall, the icefall consists of gigantic slabs of ice, or seracs, over, under or around which climbers creep. The danger is that this icefall is constantly moving, with crevasses opening up and seracs collapsing. No one can predict when or where this will happen.

A team of highly experienced sherpas, the Icefall Doctors, lay a route of ropes along which climbers navigate their way through this treacherous maze of ice. Each day, this is revisited, with climbers crossing themselves before they leave, knowing that they'd be foolish to think that luck won't play a part in getting them through safely.

The fragility of human life in the icefall was illustrated grimly in 2014, when on Everest's most fatal day 16 sherpas were killed when a towering serac collapsed.

I wish I didn't know as much as I did about the icefall. Ben tried to play it down, but on the day I knew he was

risking his life, chancing his way through Everest's pearly
gates, I instinctively reached for the only supposedly lucky
charm I have. Ben rarely returns from his travels bearing
gifts for me – he's away far too frequently for gestures like
that, and I'm far too pragmatic to want my house filled up
with knick knacks when we're paying off a mortgage.

But back in May 2017, he'd come home with a necklace. It
wasn't from him, he insisted, but from a man called Mike
with whom he'd been staying while filming New Lives in the
Wild. *A world renowned Canadian artist who had once sold*
a sculpture for a million dollars, he'd swapped his glitzy life
of success, fortune and adoration for the simple life in a
remote part of western Canada where he'd created a floating
island, a paradise where majestic cliffs fell into azure sea,
eagles fed on fish carcasses from his hands and he lived
hand-to-mouth with his wife in utopian bliss.

Ben had loved his time with this couple, marvelling at
their way of life and their inherent wisdom. As Ben prepared
to leave, Mike had thrust a necklace into his hand, telling
him that he'd made it for me, a talisman to bring me luck
while Ben ventured where few people dared. I'm not a big
jewellery wearer, I have my engagement ring and a simple
necklace that I rarely take off, but other than that, I never
wear anything else. I remember opening a black pouch to
find a piece of white-veined granite, shrouded in silver
behind which was hidden a spider. As Ben told me how
unique its maker was, I realised how extraordinary this piece
of jewellery was. Every time Ben crossed the notorious
icefall, I reached for this necklace. During idle moments I

found myself touching that piece of transparent granite, feeling its weight in my hands. I felt it was oddly reminiscent of the ice which held my husband's life so precariously in its hands and prayed that my talisman would bring me the luck Ben so desperately needed.

There's a lot of waiting around when you're preparing to summit Everest. In a world where there is so much instant gratification, where there is no waiting to receive a letter when you can send an e-mail, where a movie is instantly downloaded onto your iPad, where holiday photos can not only be instantly viewed but edited, filtered and shared with the rest of the world, this is something 21st-century climbers struggle with. This is one of the few instances where you really are at nature's mercy. You'll climb Everest when nature allows and those who dare to challenge her mostly end up regretting it.

I wanted Ben to be away for as short a time as possible, but I also wanted him to give this expedition the time it needed to give it a good chance of success. At the end of May, it was Iona's birthday, a date he'd tentatively promised he'd try and get back for. I could sense his frustration as he rode out the days at Base Camp, oscillating between baking in the high-altitude sun and freezing at night, eking out sleep in a cramped tent, perched uncomfortably on the scree below the icefall, waiting for a weather window.

The Khumbu Icefall became, in my mind, a kind of gatekeeper to the mountain. In some ways, it felt like it was the mountain's first test: are you brave, strong and determined enough to take me on, she seemed to be saying. It was Everest's way of separating the wheat from the chaff.

Shortly after we had arrived at Base Camp, we had watched as a helicopter full of climbers departed. Overwhelmed by the icefall, they had already capitulated. As I lay there in my tent, she became an ogre. A monster I had to pass before I could even begin my mountain ascent. The ice creaked and groaned as the glacier on which Base Camp is settled moved imperceptibly forward.

That night was the first of many experiences of self-doubt, as I lay in my sleeping bag picking icicles from my beard. Part of the fear and self-doubt lay in the unknown. I had no reference point. I had no idea what to expect. Was this the icy, slightly more challenging 'Go Ape' that many critics would have you believe? With the fixed line up the mountain, many have argued that Everest is little more than an adventure playground for grown-ups.

On the other hand, many described it as one of the most dangerous places in the world. Without first-hand experience, I didn't have any way of really knowing, and as is so often the case, my mind had painted the worst-case scenario. It wouldn't be long before I found out. Within the hour, we would be in the midst of the icefall. I didn't need to set an alarm. I hadn't slept a wink.

It was 4 am. The inside of the tent was covered in a thin veneer of ice formed from the condensation of my breath. You soon learned to move around the tent very gently. One bash on the side of the tent and you were showered in a blizzard of snow and ice as it sheared off the fabric and down your neck. It's not a pleasant way to get up in the mornings.

Despite instinct, I had learned over the years to sleep in as little as possible. It was always rather painful to strip off in the freezing cold and get into a cold sleeping bag. You then had to be organised enough to stuff all your clothes into your sleeping bag to keep them from freezing solid in the night.

I would often have more 'stuff' inside my sleeping bag than there was 'me'. Anything that was likely to freeze would need to be kept warm overnight. Anything left outside would be frozen solid like cardboard in the morning. It only takes one experience of frozen socks and inner boots to remember not to leave them out.

The diurnal temperature changes were truly extraordinary. By day it could be 30 °C plus, while at night it would sometimes drop to minus 15 °C. I would sit up and pull on the layers that had been scrunched down into the bottom of my sleeping bag and warmed by my body heat.

This morning, I pulled my headtorch over my woolly hat and slowly gathered everything I would need for four days up on the mountain. My breath was making such a dense heavy fog that at times I couldn't see my hand in front of my face.

I pulled my heavy boots onto my feet. My fingers were already numb with cold as I pulled a heavy down jacket over my shaking body. In the darkness, I slowly walked down to the mess tent. It felt colder in the still air of the tent than outside. Under the tiny pool of light cast by my headtorch, I pulled on my harness as I paced up and down.

I felt sick with fear and nervousness. The anxiety knotted in my stomach. It twisted and turned and made me feel physically sick. Kenton and Mark both came into the tent. Mark was fixing cameras and microphones while Kenton was uncoiling rope and fixing jumars and figures of eight. Victoria was last to arrive. Quietly, we all shuffled around in our own thoughts.

Outside the sherpas had lit the little juniper fire. I stared at the orange glow of the flame as it danced around. I scooped up a couple of handfuls of rice and threw them over the Puja. I placed some of the rice in my pocket, and, I've no idea why, some in my hair.

On the tiny stone plinth was an assortment of offerings to the mountain gods. I pulled a little packet of Jelly Babies from my bag and added it to the collection. Carefully, Kenton checked our harnesses and checked the rope. Kenton would lead followed by Victoria and then me at the back. Mark would be on his own, giving him more chance to get around to film. We wouldn't use our crampons until we reached the solid icy section of the icefall. I strapped my crampons to my rucksack, and before we knew it, we were heading off into the ice.

Base Camp is surprisingly large, and for more than 30 minutes our boots crunched over rock and ice as we passed sleeping tents. In the distance, I could make out the tiny headlamps of climbers already in the icefall. They sometimes looked like fairy lights strung together across the blackness.

Soon we crossed the little river of meltwater and we were at the base of the icefall in the Pinnacles. For what seemed like an eternity, we clambered across a mix of ice and rock as we worked our way towards the beginning of the roped icefall. An hour after leaving our Base Camp, we reached the little 'crampon area'.

Half a dozen climbers were already attaching metal spikes to their boots. By now we had also warmed up and we all shed layers. Just like the discipline of not going to bed wearing too much, we had mastered the art of dressing in the mountains, where it's a constant battle against hot and cold. Invariably, it's always too cold when you are hanging around, but as soon as you start climbing, body heat builds up, and before you know it, you are overheating. By the time you have stopped to remove layers, you are cold again.

Hot, cold, hot, cold, hot, cold.

It takes tremendous discipline to take layers off and put them back on. I sometimes found myself doing it every couple of minutes. As boring and time consuming as it was, it prevented me from either sweating or shivering to death.

I worked out the art of taking layers on and off without even stopping. I would slip one arm out of my rucksack and then pull an arm from my jacket or fleece, before slipping my arm back into the rucksack. I would then repeat it on the other side, before tying whatever I had removed around my waist. I sometimes found myself walking with up to three garments tied around my waist.

Scarf on. Scarf off. Hat on. Hat off.

A single rope stretched across the icy path ahead. One by one, we each clipped our carabiner onto the fixed line. Sheer cliffs of ice towered above us as we worked our way up a thin path. It was like walking up a narrow street. Our crampons gripped into the snow and ice. The path zig-zagged up a shallow gradient which soon began to increase. Steps became bigger and the going was harder. My torch could only make out the immediate area, but it was difficult to work out where we were or what we were heading into.

It was probably a good thing, as it was about to get a whole lot harder. The rope soon soared up a sheer cliff of ice, perhaps 20 metres high. By now there was a small queue of climbers ahead of us. I had, of course, heard about the mountain queues that built up at these bottlenecks, but this was my first experience of it, along with the realisation that I would soon be one of those climbers holding up everyone behind me.

I watched as all those around me tut-tutted and criticised the technique or lack of ability of those ahead of us and had the sudden dawning realisation that I was about to be observed myself. It wasn't hard, or even high, but this little ice wall was about to test my own technical abilities; after all, even with two years of preparation, I was still a relative novice compared to many.

I clipped my jumar to the rope and dug the toes of my crampons into the ice. With all my strength, I hauled the jumar as high as it would go and then lifted my legs higher. I was terrified of failing to get the crampons into the ice properly and slipping.

Surprisingly, it wasn't the fear of falling that worried me but the fear of humiliating myself in front of my peers. These were climbers with whom I would be sharing the mountain for the next couple of weeks.

'Focus,' I berated myself as I hauled the jumar up the rope. I wasn't kicking hard enough and I could feel the weakness of my foothold. It wouldn't be able to hold my weight. Panic surged through me and I struggled to catch my breath. For the first time in the whole journey from Lukla, I lost my breath, and the more I panicked the worse it became.

It was a feeling of being out of my depth. The negative voice in my head had appeared, and for the first, and certainly not the last time, the doubts settled in. I was too inexperienced. I berated myself. I wasn't up to it. Everyone around me appeared to be veteran climbers with years of experience under their belt.

It's amazing how the panic can spread both physically and mentally. I was overcome with what I can only describe as doom. It's like the whole body just gives up trying. It's like you have given in to the darkness and allow the negativity to flood through you. It steals your breath. My heart was racing. I wanted to lie down and give up. Most of all, I wanted to click my boot heels together and return home.

Except I didn't really. The negative voice is all part of the Everest challenge. How to drown it out, how to silence and control it, are part of the second-by-second struggle of climbing the mountain.

In the past, I've been able to draw on previous experiences. I thought back to the time I jumped in with the crocodiles. The time we capsized on the Atlantic. I tried to draw the dark clouds from my mind and replace them with the bright light of hope and confidence.

'You can do this, Ben,' I repeated in my head.

'Just focus,' I repeated over and over.

I managed to ascend the small wall of ice. I collapsed on the top, unable to move. I had to crawl from the edge on all fours. Breathless and sweaty, things weren't looking good. How did the others do? Fine. I regained my composure and we were off again through the meandering field of ice. We zig-zagged around huge blocks of ice until we reached our first ladder.

The ladders of Everest are almost as famous as the mountain itself. Sometimes with up to four ladders all lashed taut, they are used as temporary bridges to span the crevasses that cut across the icefall like lightning bolts. These crevasses can be hundreds of feet deep and 20 feet wide. The ladders have been used for many years as an easily adjustable way of breaching and crossing the huge gaps and fissures that spread across the icefall like veins.

As the glacier shifts, so too does the icefall. Crevasses open and close, widen and narrow. The ladders are put in place by an expert team of sherpas called the Icefall Doctors, who traverse the route daily, adding new ladders and ropes through the ice.

Our first crevasse was about 10 feet wide, enough to need two aluminium ladders lashed together in the middle with ropes. Two guide ropes, onto which we could clip safety lines attached to our harnesses, stretched across the gap. These safety lines would stop us from disappearing into the depths of the crevasse and certain death.

There was little chance of surviving a fall into one of these bottomless cracks in the ice. Instant death would certainly be preferable to surviving a fall and ending up in the cavernous depths, hundreds of feet beneath a glacier and far from any chance of rescue. It used to make me shiver just thinking about it.

Very carefully, I clipped my safety lines onto the guide ropes and gingerly placed one foot on the ladder.

Have you ever tried walking across a horizontal ladder? Probably not, because they are much easier to climb when vertical, which is what they are made for. Traversing a horizontal ladder is one thing, but try doing it wearing clunky boots with crampons, in the dark, across a seemingly bottomless drop, in thin, oxygen-deprived air and it's a whole other challenge.

My size 12 boots were large enough to span the gap between rungs, but the crampons were spaced to wedge nicely between them too. It meant that each step locked my foot into the ladder like a Lego brick. It took quite a force to pull it from the rungs. If I pulled too hard, I risked falling off balance and plunging into the abyss.

I took a step. Staring ahead of me, heart racing, I have never focused so hard as I lifted one foot in front of the other. The two ladders began to bow and wobble as I reached the rudimentary rope that lashed the two together in the middle. I could feel a bead of sweat on my brow.

My left foot wouldn't budge. My crampon had wedged itself hard against one of the ropes. I couldn't lift it from the ladder. I didn't want to look down, but I needed to see what had happened. A small pool of torchlight illuminated the sides of the icy crevasse. I felt dizzy. I wriggled my foot free and carefully made my way across the rest of the ladder. I leapt the final rung. I wanted to kiss the ground. The relief of getting off that ladder was overwhelming. I felt a buzz of endorphins and euphoria. It was surprisingly uplifting for 5 am.

By now the faint outline of dawn had painted the horizon with a soft hue of pink. Daybreak was quick to follow and within 15 minutes there was no longer any need for a headtorch. The reflection of the early morning sky in the snow and ice was dazzling even at 5.15 am.

With dawn came the realisation of where we were. I could clearly make out Base Camp. It was 'right there', seemingly within touching distance. It hardly felt like we had made any headway at all; what's more, I could now make out the magnitude of this icy world. I could see every drop, every hole, crevasse and fin of ice. If you took a great slab of snow and ice and dropped it on the floor, then did it again, and then again, this is what it would resemble.

We continued to weave and meander through the icy obstacle course, through our own little maze, over more crevasses, some needing just a single ladder, others demanding three ladders roped together that swayed with each step. Sometimes the ladders went upwards, other times they went down steeply. Sometimes they were lashed vertically against a cliff face.

Up, down, in, out, we weaved. By now we were alone in the icefall. Halfway up is an area known as the football field. It was the only area in the icefall wide enough to stop for a sip of tea and some Haribo.

We didn't stop for long. We still had several hours of climbing and we were about to reach the most dangerous part of the Khumbu Icefall.

As the icefall narrows nearer to Camp 1, the route trails perilously close to the side where enormous seracs, huge walls of unstable ice, cling. It's the collapse of these vulnerable and unsecure seracs that causes the frequent avalanches in the Khumbu Valley.

I watched as Kenton looked above us and shook his head, 'Right, no stopping, no filming. I want everyone to get through here as fast as possible.' I learned to watch Kenton and Mark in much the same way that I observe the crew on a plane when there is turbulence. If they continue chatting with one another, unaffected, then I relax. One glimmer of fear and you know you're in trouble.

For the first time on the mountain, I saw concern in their eyes.

The temperature had plunged, down to minus 20 °C. Kenton had warned us that 6 am is the coldest time of the day in the Khumbu and he wasn't wrong. It was bitterly cold. I could feel the freezing wind chafing my cheeks. This was frostbite weather. Exposed skin freezes and the cells die. I pulled my buff high up onto my face and pulled my hat down close to my sunglasses – the sun's glare off the ice and snow was intense.

We were shattered and freezing as we finally summited a narrow ridgeline and spotted a small cluster of tents in the distance – Camp 1. Up and down a series of leg-sapping undulations in the glacier and we finally reached the windswept tents. Camp 1 is more of a transit camp. Climbers, like us, use it to acclimatise during their first rotation, but after that it is merely a stopping point on the way to the better organised and resourced Camp 2, further up the valley. The camp had a temporary feeling. I counted about 20 tents.

Ant and Ed, who had arrived the day before us, were still wrapped up in their sleeping bags against the chill. As we would be 'hot bedding', we had to wait for them to get up, pack and leave before we could get into the tent ourselves. We had to pace up and down, stomping our feet and swinging our arms to keep the cold at bay. I marched up and down the tiny camp trying to keep the blood flowing through my chilled body. The sweat that had dampened my thermal layers during the strenuous climb was chilling me to the core.

The wind had picked up and the temperature had plummeted still further. It was 8 am and I couldn't wait for the comparative warmth and protection of the tent. Ed and Ant weren't in a rush to pack up. I couldn't blame them, but I wanted to throttle them.

With the bitter wind, it felt pretty inhospitable. Victoria had gone ahead of me in the ascent and had arrived before me. Numbed from the cold, she had started showing the first signs of hypothermia. She was shaking violently, and her lips were blue. Although I was cold, I was surprised at how badly she had reacted.

Finally, Ed and Ant emerged from the tent and we were able to bundle Victoria into her sleeping bag. I crawled into the little tent next to her and pulled off my heavy boots. It had only taken us five hours to get through the icefall, but I felt emotionally and physically drained, and now I was concerned for Victoria.

With our little stove we melted some snow to make a warm cup of tea sweetened with sugar. You'll never really appreciate the full qualities of a hot cuppa until you are in a tent up at 6,000 metres in the Himalayas.

The wind beat at our tent with its ice-cold sting. It was still early morning and I couldn't wait for the heat of the sun's rays to warm us up. I didn't need to wait for long. From the ice-encrusted minus 20 °C of the morning, the tent transformed from igloo to sauna. The intensity of the sun was astonishing as her ferocious rays built the temperature in the tent up to nearly 35 °C. I lay there in my underwear, sweating. We opened all the vents and doors and used our sleeping bags to drape over the top of the tent to try and make a sunscreen, which worked surprisingly well.

I never expected the heat to be so overpowering as I lay there sweltering and sweating. Occasionally, it became too much and I would spring from the tent into the dazzling white snow. Even outside, the power of the rays was so intense that after just a few minutes, I needed to retreat back into the tent.

A warm cup of tea and the heat had revived Victoria from her hypothermia, but now she was feeling the early effects of altitude sickness. She had a banging headache and was feeling nauseous. Although unsurprising at 6,000 metres of elevation, the intensity of her symptoms was worrying Kenton.

We decided to give her supplementary oxygen. Most climbers don't require extra O's (as oxygen is known on the mountain) until they reach Camp 3 at 7,000 metres, almost a vertical kilometre above us, and although it is often administered as a medicine at intervals to revive and alleviate symptoms, it was certainly a concern that at such an early stage, Victoria already required extra oxygen.

We also had to account for extra usage. Getting bottled oxygen to key points up and down the mountain was crucial to the success of our expedition. Known as caches, these drop-off points had to be carefully planned to ensure enough oxygen for the whole team.

Victoria and I dozed and chatted through the heat of the day. We ate a rehydrated meal and played cards until the sun went down, and with it the oven-like heat replaced by a freezer-like chill. From sweating in my underpants less than an hour before, I found myself shivering inside my summit sleeping bag.

None of us slept much that night. I had my first experience of altitude-induced sleep apnoea – in a particular form known as Cheyne-Stokes respiration. Every time I dozed off, I found myself waking up, unable to breathe. It felt like I was

The team's first climb in Bolivia (Victoria, Kenton and me).

With Victoria at the summit of Illimani – the highest mountain in Bolivia (6,438 metres).

Ludo and Iona wave me off from Colombo airport in Sri Lanka. Leaving my family for this challenge was one of the hardest things I have ever done.

Trekking to Everest in holiday clothes. My bags had been sent somewhere other than Kathmandu.

Victoria and I take a tour with the Red Cross to see some of the good work they are doing in the region.

I invited my father-in-law, Jonathan Hunt, to join us on the trek to Base Camp. He offered me some spare pants – 10 days in the same underwear is not great for team bonding.

Prayer flags are everywhere on the trek to Base Camp. Getting chilly enough to borrow a jacket – my bags had still not turned up.

Mark Fisher, our cameraman, joined our team late in the day. Here are all five of us on the way to Base Camp (Victoria, Jonathan, me, Kenton and Mark).

Shorts and a jaunty hat – not the usual outfit for the trek to Base Camp.

Dwarfed by the immense and majestic landscape.

With our team of sherpas (Ang Phurba Sherpa, Siddhi Tamang, Jenjen Lama, me, Phree Chombi Sherpa and Pemba Sherpa). I loved spending time with these people – they love the mountain and showed us the way to treat her with respect. Without the sherpas, climbing Everest would be almost impossible for amateurs like me.

A common noise at Base Camp is the unnerving 'BOOM' of avalanches. The danger is real and constant.

Leaving Camp 2 on one of our pre-summit 'rotations' to the higher camps. Climbers acclimatise to the thinner air gradually before pushing on to the summit.

Kenton scales an 'ice fin' in the Khumbu Icefall.

Proper mountaineering at an ice wall between Camps 1 and 2. Walls like this test your physical and mental strength.

Crevasses on Everest can be hundreds of feet deep and more than twenty feet across. They must be treated with extreme caution.

'Always look up,' my grandmother used to say. With spectacular scenery and light like this, who wouldn't?

Prayer flags adorn the mountain – they remind you of what a spiritual journey scaling Everest can be.

Oxygen tanks waiting to go up the mountain. Climbing Everest without oxygen is only for the very few. The rest of us couldn't survive without it.

Another night at Camp 2 awaiting our next rotation up the mountain.

An intense climb to get to Camp 4.

In the death zone, you need a constant supply of oxygen to help you climb and breathe. Climbers have to limit their time up here as much as possible. The air at 7,600 metres and above is so thin that prolonged exposure to the conditions there can have serious consequences for your physical and mental health.

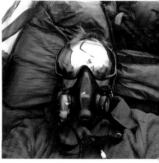

A storm raged while we were at Camp 4 before the summit attempt. We were sheltering in flimsy tents being attacked by wind that was the most violent and angry I have ever experienced. It was a very long night.

Clipped onto the vital rope line, and with my oxygen mask in place, I am ready to make my way up to the roof of the world.

A pause in the ascent. I wanted to experience a few steps without oxygen so that I could 'feel' the mountain and the raw challenge. Not long after my oxygen regulator failed and I was in real danger.

At the south summit, each step is a struggle. Even with oxygen the physical effort of putting one foot in front of the other is immense.

Tackling the Hillary Step, which in 2018 had been nearly completely covered in snow, so was more the 'Hillary Slope'.

The final push to the summit. Despite every kind of problem – meteorological, physical and manmade – the top of the world was in our sights.

The summit!

The highest selfie you can take.

One of the proudest moments of my life: Ludo and Iona's favourite toys enjoy the view.

The view from the top.

Kenton told me that I should save 25–30 per cent of my strength and energy for the descent. After the euphoria of summiting, the descent is even more dangerous than the ascent.

The trip down is hazardous,
so keeping your focus is vital.

Back at Base Camp for a final group picture (me, Kenton and Mark). We did it!

Home with Marina and my wonderful children. In the end, you do what you do to show your children what is possible, to inspire them to push themselves as far as they can go.

My daughter's diary entry. I may have 'smelt of rotten cheese,' but at least I was home.

drowning or suffocating. It is deeply, deeply unpleasant and the worry had a spiralling effect on my ability to sleep, to the point that I became genuinely fearful of sleeping in case I suffocated to death.

We were only at Camp 1, nearly three vertical kilometres from the summit, and Vic and I were both already struggling. Morning couldn't come soon enough, and in the frozen chill of dawn, before the sun's heat took effect, we headed off towards Camp 2, just 400 metres up the valley.

I was surprised by how exhausting and draining that short distance was to cover. The gradient was disarmingly shallow. It looked like a breeze, but by the time Camp 2 came into view, I felt like I had done several rounds in the boxing ring.

We could see the camp for hours before we arrived. It was spread out along the side of the valley, tantalising us, but we never seemed to get any closer. It was agonisingly slow progress as we inched our way up the valley. By now the sun had reached full intensity and sapped us further of our energy.

Finally, we reached the first tent, but as we would soon learn on Everest, nothing is as it seems. It would take more than an hour and a half to climb through Camp 2 to the upper part where we were based.

That climb seemed to go on forever. Frequently forced to stop and sit down from exhaustion, I was very nearly defeated. Not that I had any option. As was so often the case here, the only way was up.

The relief of finally reaching our little encampment was overwhelming, and once again a cup of sweet tea brought me back to life. In the small mess tent were the rest of the climbers with

whom we'd shared Base Camp. They were an eclectic mix of individuals. There was a 20-year-old tech billionaire, a hedge fund
manager and a CIA agent, as well as ex-SBS soldier Ant and
cameraman Ed.

They were all squashed into this little tent watching *The
Revenant* on an iPad. It seemed a strange choice of film to watch
at 6,400 metres, but it was a welcome distraction from the
increased altitude and the reduced oxygen in the thin air.

We spent the next day resting and acclimatising while the rest
of the group descended. Ed and Ant had decided to try for Camp
3 on their first rotation. By doing so, they were hoping that they
could try for the summit on their second rotation rather than the
third. It was a risky bid, and one that Kenton wasn't prepared to
try with us.

High-altitude climbing requires time and patience and Kenton
wanted to maximise our chances of success with as much acclimatisation as we could get. To avoid languishing in the sauna-like
tents, Kenton had suggested a short climb to the base of the
Lhotse Face, on the wall of which Camp 3 is cut into a ledge.

We made a leisurely stroll up to its vertiginous wall. It looked
terrifying. Once again, I was reminded of the Wall in *Game of
Thrones*. It was here that Kenton had found a sherpa hanging
from his safety rope with half his head missing. The experience
had affected him deeply after he had recovered the body. No one
ever really understood what had happened, and Kenton assumed
it was a freak accident in which he had been hit on the head by a
large piece of rock or ice.

We returned to Camp 2 for a rest and some food. Once again,
I found myself suffering from sleep apnoea. What would happen

if I had this all the way to the summit? I wasn't sure I could sustain my mental and physical capabilities on so little sleep.

It was about 4 pm when things started going wrong. Victoria and I were in the tent together. She had been sleeping, but now she was sitting bolt upright. Her face was pale, her eyes sunken. She stared blankly into the distance, holding her hands to her temples. She complained of an unbearable headache and she seemed confused. I fished around in my bag for the pulse oximeter, I clipped it to her finger, and it read 38 per cent. It had to be wrong. I tried it again. This time it read 35 per cent. A 'normal' reading would be between 95 and 100 per cent, indicating normal levels of oxygen saturation in the blood. Anything under 90 per cent is considered 'low'. When it dips below 84 per cent, in the words of one online analysis, 'it's time to go to hospital'.

I was sure it must be broken, so tried it on my finger. It read 89 per cent. Again, I clipped it to Victoria's: 36 per cent. I reached for her bottle of oxygen and pulled the mask onto her face and cranked up the flow rate to its maximum and then went to get Kenton. He was in the mess tent with Mark, playing cards with Ant and Ed.

As I was explaining my concern to Kenton, Victoria unzipped the tent and stumbled through the doorway. Unable to control her balance, she lurched and swayed like a drunk before collapsing on the floor.

'It feels like knitting needles are being stuck into my brain,' she stammered. She was slurring her words.

'My oxygen saturation was 29 per cent.'

'WHAT?!' gasped Kenton.

I looked at the shocked faces around us and ran to our tent to fetch the oxygen cylinder and mask. Again, we strapped it to her face and Kenton poured some medicine into her mouth. I sat there on the tent floor holding her hand. She was suffering acute mountain sickness and we had to get her down the mountain as quickly as possible.

It was too late to begin a night-time descent. With supplementary oxygen and Acetazolamide – the go-to drug to prevent and reduce the symptoms of altitude sickness – she would stabilise, but we had to make a rapid departure at first light to get back to Base Camp where she could get medical help.

A mixture of sleep apnoea and concern for Victoria meant I didn't sleep that night.

Had we taken a risk too far?

Risk is a strange thing. It's something we, as a society, have largely tried to expunge and eradicate. It is often hidden behind the façade of Health and Safety, but in reality it is much bigger than that. I could eulogise about 'when I was a boy', but to be honest our risk-averse culture is far older than that. In some ways, risk comes with humanity. We all take some form of risk on a daily basis, only we now use technology to mitigate and minimise those risks. Risk of course comes in many different forms: financial, work, relationships, to name just a few, but of course it is the risk of injury or death of which we are arguably most fearful. Some people make careers out of confronting risk. Miners, deep-sea trawlermen, soldiers, police … you get my point. And there are also sports like Formula One and mountaineering where the risk of death is ever present. Risk is still out there despite what we have done to try and tame it.

The problem comes down to who sets the criteria for risks and their management. When governments do it, we blame the 'nanny state', and when schools do it we blame "elf and safety".

Another strange symptom of society is our need to justify everything we do. Back in the heroic days of exploration, it was all done for King and country. I don't think you'd get away with it today – 'doing it for Queen and country' doesn't cut the mustard anymore. When asked why he was trying to climb Everest, George Mallory famously answered 'because it's there'. Of course, this quote needs to be taken in the context of the time. He had just returned from the horrors of World War I; had lost friends and in many respects his old life. For Mallory, the mountain provided a focus and a reason to live.

Today, society expects a reasonable and, preferably, worthy cause. After all, Everest has been climbed many times. And people justifiably have questions. 'What are you adding?' 'What makes your climb unique?' A lot of the time your answers to these questions are greeted with a dismissive, 'So what?'

Well, I disagree. I think every adventure, every journey, every challenge is unique to the individual.

The challenges, the adversity, the fear, the dangers, the pain, the dreams, the elation are all uniquely different. Every climb of Everest is different and personal.

Every climber has their own reasons for being there. You don't have to be the first, or the fastest, or the youngest, or the tallest, or the oldest. You just need to dream. And achieving a dream is never without risk.

Risk is all about perception. The risk scale varies greatly, from walking down the street with the risk of falling over, through to being hit by a car or being mugged, to the extreme of full hand-to-hand combat in a war zone. But why take risks in the first place? For me, it's the only way to grow or make progress. If we stick within the safety parameters of our comfort zone, then how can we ever improve? The greater the risk, the bigger the return.

So what do we stand to gain? For a start, it invariably opens up new opportunities. Taking risks empowers you to stretch the boundaries of what you know and are comfortable with. It empowers you to think bigger and be bolder; it allows you to achieve higher goals.

Risks encourage quick thinking, creativity and resourcefulness. I'm a strong believer in the power of the mind: a positive attitude will invariably help create a positive outcome. It's impossible to plan every step in your life. When you take a risk, you are more likely to try harder and give it your best.

Taking risks helps you to clearly define what you really want. Calculated risks are taken with careful thought. Yet the fact that you are taking a risk pushes you to make things work. Surely you will first have to determine if the reward is something you want enough to take the chance. If it is, then move ahead and don't look back.

Once you have become desensitised and accustomed to taking risks, you break free from the manacles of society and expectation. You become braver and bolder; self-confidence and self-esteem grow and create a stronger mindset.

Taking the first step is always the hardest. I think humans are instinctively risk averse. We like habit and consistency. If we strip it back to the very bare, basic needs in life, these are shelter, food and water. In some ways, these are all we need.

For the past five years, I have travelled the globe meeting risk takers who have abandoned the conventions of society and broken free from the shackles of the material world to embrace a brave new life in the wild, living off-grid. Effectively, each of these individuals has decided to make a conscious decision to shun conventional society for what is arguably a simpler, though riskier life. By embracing a world where their only needs are food, water and shelter, they have certainly simplified their life needs, but it doesn't necessarily make it easier.

During that time, I have met so many different people who have adopted this new life: from a Miami taxi driver who moved to a palm hut in the Philippines, to the modern white tribe of 'freetarians' who live off the food left in rubbish bins in the Appalachian Mountains of North America. Each one is unique and different; the one unifying characteristic was their happiness, often in the face of adversity.

In the city, for most people access to food, shelter and water is relatively easy. Even those who are struggling financially can have access to foodbanks, homeless shelters and water, but in the wilderness these can often be the difference between life and death. You only need to look at the story of Christopher McCandless, the ideological law student who quit his Ivy League education in pursuit of a simpler life off-grid in Alaska. I don't want to be the spoiler for those who haven't read the book but … he ate some poisoned berries and died. Death of course is the worst-case scenario for any risk taker.

It was Ernest Hemingway who once wrote that the only real sports were motor racing, bull fighting and mountaineering. It's an interesting observation. He was implying that they were more 'heroic' as the risk of death was greater than that of, say, football or tennis.

I have always been fascinated by 'perceived' risk. My wife will sometimes obsess over something seemingly risk free. Before heading to Everest, on our family holiday in Sri Lanka, she would always worry about me running along the road each day for my exercise. For those who have been to Sri Lanka, it is a fair worry, but to mitigate that risk, I would always run against the traffic so that I controlled the situation. I could watch the cars, buses and lorries from a distance and was always ready to jump into a ditch or a hedge.

What surprised me more was my wife's worry. I have done far riskier things, but in Marina's eyes, this was pretty dangerous. Surprisingly, she never made a fuss when I went scuba diving with crocodiles, which I think is quite high on the risk scale.

The crocodile example is quite an interesting one. It came shortly after I became a father for the second time. Iona had just been born and Ludo was a little over a year old. Being a father is my greatest responsibility. I would honestly drop everything for my children. The realisation in the middle of the Okavango Delta of my vulnerability underwater, with no protection, just a few inches from one of Africa's apex predators, was profound and certainly led to a period of soul-searching. I found it particularly hard, because this was the kind of risk on which I thrived.

I am really not a very brave person. There are plenty of things I would be far too scared to try. I have never bungee jumped, and

I never will, but this is why risk is so nuanced. For some people, risk is a financial thing; for others risk is about pride. There is risk of rejection; risk of financial loss; risk of humiliation; risk of failure; risk of fear. The list goes on and on.

My point is that without risk we cannot grow. We cannot improve. We cannot learn. We cannot experience. Without some form of risk, we are in danger of never really living. Can we ever really be ourselves if we don't take risks?

Without risk I wouldn't be the person I am today – it's a big part of me. As a boy I was incredibly shy, and I mean 'couldn't look anyone in the eyes' kind of shy. I lacked confidence and self-esteem. I hated my shyness. Inside was the extrovert, the son of an actress, but outside was a shy little boy uncomfortable in his own skin. It probably didn't help that I wasn't much good at anything. Hopeless at sport and unacademic, I didn't really know where to channel the person within.

One day I woke up and decided to do an assembly on my own in front of the whole school. Now just take a moment to think about this. Me, the shy quiet boy who was embarrassed in front of my own reflection in the mirror, had decided to do an assembly in front of 700 pupils and staff, most of them many years older than me.

I was 15 and decided to do a comedy routine. I am blushing just thinking about it. I even learned a song. I honestly have no idea where the bravery to do that assembly came from. The risks were huge. I risked humiliation in front of the whole school.

On my current risk scale, I would put it at 9/10. Despite my job, I am not an extrovert. I never have been and never will be, so the risk of becoming a laughing stock in front of my friends with whom I would be spending the next three years was a pretty big one.

But I did it. On reflection, it was probably my first step towards Everest. I can still remember the nerves, the fear, the trepidation. It was the first time I had knowingly stepped out of my comfort zone into the unknown. I don't remember much of it, but I will never forget the applause at the end. It was so empowering. Like I say, the bigger the risk, the bigger the gain. The thing is, society wants the gains without the risks.

Type 'risk' into an online search engine and you will be provided with dozens of pages about risk management and risk mitigation. Society has become risk averse. We often try to eradicate risk entirely.

We could put this down to the increasingly litigious 'blame culture' world where you are only a 'trip on the pavement' away from suing or being sued; or maybe it is the mollycoddled world in which we wrap our children to shield them from risk.

Whatever the cause, we are increasingly risk averse. Perhaps it is one of the reasons we marvel at racing drivers or the derring-do of adventurers. We worship those who take risks because we are too fearful to take them ourselves.

What's more, society has become increasingly pessimistic. News seems to be skewed towards negativity. The result is often that people will look at the worst-case scenario first. If we flipped this attitude, I feel sure people would feel more empowered to take more risks. For most of us, risk is simply the unknown, and that, in my mind, is what makes it so exciting.

As a father, I now have to juggle my own approach to risk while also balancing my children's. On the one hand, I want to nurture and protect them, but on the other hand I also want to encourage them to push themselves out of their comfort zone. As parents, whether we like it or not, we are role models to our children. We lead by example.

If we always take the easy option, where is the challenge? It was this epiphany in which the Everest project was born.

Marina – Risk

The trouble with big expeditions is that they take a long time to organise. I spent most of 2017 saying in answer to questions about whether I was worried, 'I'm sure I will be, when the time comes.' While Ben started training expeditions and our house slowly filled up with high-altitude mountain kit, I still regarded the expedition as too far in the future to worry about.

And then I overheard a conversation between my son Ludo and his friend. Ben announced his expedition and from then that's all everyone wanted to talk about. 'You know your Daddy will probably die on Everest,' piped up an eight-year-old classmate who had recently watched the film, Everest, where (in this boy's defence) most of them did die. Before I could intervene, Ludo responded cheerily, 'No, don't worry, my Daddy definitely won't die.' I realised it was time to have a frank chat with our children.

Ben and I have always been on the same page when it comes to risk. We are both fierce believers that a life with no risk is a life not worth living. You do what you can to make sure your life is long enough to benefit from the richness that this world brings, but you don't become so risk averse that it stops allowing you to have any fun.

Parents in the 21st century are consumed with worry. It starts with pregnancy, the conflicting advice about what you can and can't eat, the scaremongering articles in the media about terrible things that happen to babies and children – the mother's kiss that killed her baby (a cold sore), the toxic paint on the cot. We bring our children into a world where they have to sit in a car seat until they are 14, of sterilisers and where we 'baby proof' our houses and disinfect every surface. We are catapulted into a world in which risk is considered bad.

The problem is that it's not real life. Children are constantly exploring, touching, feeling, licking. They are pushing their boundaries to see where those boundaries are. If they hurt themselves, it's a surefire way of teaching them never to make the same mistake again. But if we don't let them make mistakes, we're robbing them of the opportunity to learn.

Which is why Ben and I are happy for our children to climb trees and sometimes fall out of them. Our children's knees are etched with an ever-evolving catalogue of scratches and grazes. There's often a bruise or two somewhere, but they're also careful and respectful of their environment.

In this context it makes it easier to justify their Daddy's expedition. One car journey, we talked to them about how exciting climbing Everest was going to be. They needed no convincing. 'I just can't wait for you to climb Everest,' Ludo enthused. But we also talked about the risks. We told them that it was dangerous, that many people have died trying to climb the mountain and that everyone who goes risks their lives. But we also talked about what you can do to mitigate those risks and likened it to everyday life.

We'd recently returned from a blissful skiing holiday which encapsulated the idea perfectly. I reminded them how much fun it was to ski off piste, racing through the powder, in between the trees, following my sister (a ski instructor) like a trail of adrenaline-fuelled ducklings, but I also reminded them how wearing a helmet to do this was non-negotiable.

The trouble is that life, whatever stage you're at, without risk is not worth living. Having lost a baby before he got to experience the richness of our world, I feel that if we are lucky enough to get a go at life on this planet, it is our duty to enjoy it. And that involves taking risk.

The writer, William Arthur Ward sums this up perfectly. 'To love is to risk not being loved in return, to live is to risk dying, to hope is to risk despair, to try is to risk failure. But risks must be taken because the greatest hazard in life is to risk nothing. The person who risks nothing, does nothing, has nothing, is nothing.'

While our opinions differ on many occasions, when it comes to risk, Ben's and my perspectives are perfectly aligned. We live life to the full, taking opportunities and the inevitable risks that a life full of adventure presents. We feel that if our children have a similar attitude, seizing opportunity, pushing themselves out of their comfort zone and reaping the buzz, the joy and the excitement that come with that, then we've done a good job as parents.

Victoria lay in the tent trembling from the cold. Her whole body was shaking violently in her sleeping bag. I could hear her laboured breathing and her lips were a light shade of blue.

'Are you okay, Vic?'

I looked around and could see fear on Kenton's face. The gravity of the situation became obvious. I didn't sleep that night. I lay awake next to Victoria listening for any change in her breathing. I was terrified she would stop breathing or suffer some sort of seizure. The morning couldn't come soon enough.

CHAPTER NINE

DIFFERENT ENDINGS

At daybreak we began the descent. By now Victoria was on her feet again, and with the help of several bottles of oxygen, she had bounced back. To the untrained eye she looked completely normal, but Kenton and I knew it was the supplementary oxygen and the medicine speaking. It was both unsustainable and dangerous to carry on. We knew it, but Victoria was in denial as to the severity of the situation and was convinced that all she needed was a short recovery before she carried on.

From high up in Camp 2, we began the long journey to Base Camp. For nearly an hour, we yomped through the tents that were scattered across Camp 2 until we reached the long valley to Camp 1 and the top of the icefall.

Descending, the trek was easy. It seemed hard to believe; on the ascent, this had felt like a never-ending slope. The gentle elevation had felt like purgatory. I had been surprised by how demoralising it had felt.

We wound our way past yawning crevasses until we reached the vertical 20-metre wall of ice that had caused such a bottleneck on the way up. I clipped on my figure of eight and gently lowered myself down that sheer cliff of ice. Soon we were back at Camp 1 and it was time to descend back through the unstable labyrinth of snow and ice.

'There was a huge ice collapse last night,' warned a climber coming up through the maze. 'Three sherpas fell into a crevasse,' another explained. 'The whole route has shifted.'

'It's pretty scary,' an experienced climber added helpfully.

My heart sank. Three sherpas … It soon transpired that they had been rescued and had already been helicoptered off the mountain, their injuries unknown. At least they had survived. But now we had to climb through the volatile icefall that had nearly taken their lives and navigate through the recently collapsed fall. As if the climb hadn't been daunting enough, I now felt a renewed sense of doom as we clambered beneath the teetering seracs that threatened to collapse at any moment.

'Don't stop,' Kenton urged looking concerned, 'don't even clip onto the rope unless you have to.'

While controversial, his advice made sense to me. Haste here was more important than being clipped on. Of course, I would make sure my safety harness was tethered when crossing ladders and for the more exposed parts of the descent, but for much of it, I used common sense … and speed.

It wasn't long before we reached the icefall. Half a dozen empty packs, left by the sherpas who had been involved in the collapse and subsequent rescue, had been tied to the rope. They were a haunting reminder of our mortality. I couldn't help but imagine the fear and terror they must have felt on this very spot just a couple of hours before.

A new series of ladders had already been installed by the Icefall Doctors, to bridge the gaping new holes and crevasses that had formed. One section was creating a bottleneck. A steep descent led to a horizontal ladder that led onto a vertical ladder that bridged a gap at a steep angle. Beyond this was a roped section up a vertiginous fin of ice. In the middle was the rubble from the ice collapse. It was a pretty terrifying clamber.

Victoria and Kenton went first, followed by Mark and me. Mark remained on the high cliff to film me as I scaled the impressive fin of ice. As scary as it was, it was also quite dramatic and spectacular. Just below me, at the bottom of the fin, I could see Kenton and Victoria.

I clipped my ascender onto the rope and just as I took my first step, I heard a mighty boom, like thunder followed by a long low grumble. I looked at Mark who had his back turned to me. He was facing the mountain and a wall of snow and ice that was tumbling down and cascading towards us.

One of the seracs had been released, unleashing a vast avalanche that was racing down the steep slope in our direction.

Life went into slow motion. I watched Mark, closest to the avalanche, as he paced back and forth looking for somewhere safe. He was on a cliff edge with nowhere to shelter, nothing to hide behind. I watched in horror as he realised his vulnerability.

My attention turned to Kenton and Victoria. I could see Kenton but for one horrible moment there was no sign of Vic. I soon realised he was on top of her. He was using his body to shield her from the impact of the avalanche.

It's strange how people react in a moment of extreme danger when your very life is in jeopardy. When James Cracknell and I had capsized in the Atlantic Ocean, thousands of miles from land, I had found myself in open water, without a life jacket or safety harness and with just an upturned boat. I felt sure I was heading to meet my maker. Strangely, there was no fear, just a resignation of death. I felt slightly annoyed at myself for letting it happen, and then I noticed some barnacles that had grown on the underside of the boat.

During our journey, James had insisted that we get into the shark-infested waters every couple of days to scrape off the barnacles, the presence of which, in James's mind, would otherwise slow us down.

'How did we miss those barnacles?' I wondered, as I surveyed the upturned hull and prepared to die.

Here on Everest, I was watching as an avalanche raced towards us – all in slow motion. The rumble of snow and ice reverberated through me. It rose like a moving beast as the thinner, lighter snow at the front billowed up in a threatening cloud.

I marvelled at Kenton's heroism and then glanced up at Mark who looked like a rabbit in car headlights. I stood rooted to the spot. There was nothing to do. I just hoped it would be quick. The avalanche continued to speed towards us and I felt the cold wind and snow of the snout. I closed my eyes and waited for impact.

Nothing.

I opened my eyes and there was no sign of Mark, just a huge cloud of powdery snow. As the dust settled, Mark was still standing there, on top of that cliff, rooted to the spot.

The avalanche had stopped just a few metres from us. It was pure luck that we hadn't been any higher and that there hadn't been enough weight or speed in the avalanche to reach us. I wiped the snow and ice from my face and in stunned silence we carried on down through the icefall. The unflappable Mark looked shell shocked. He had been closest to the impact and he had been sure it would reach us.

The avalanche had been another reminder of the inherent risks of being here and of the lottery of passing through the icefall. I felt a sickness deep within as we continued our descent towards the comparative safety of Base Camp below.

The relief as we reached the tents was palpable. We were worn ragged from the thin air, and the endurance-sapping physical stress of the climb and the draining emotion of fear and vulnerability had taken a huge toll on all of us. When the entire climbing party got back to Base Camp, we retreated to our tents to recover.

At altitude high up in the mountains, you grow accustomed to suffering. In some ways, you become desensitised to it. Headaches and nausea become the norm. It has always amazed me how quickly we adapt to a new routine or environment. We humans are pretty astonishing with our chameleon-like ability to blend in with a new environment. No matter the desert, the ocean, a jungle, caves: we have an ability to adapt and overcome.

Mountains, and Everest in particular, are often described as a 'suffer-fest' – if you can put up with the suffering then your chances of success are pretty high. The thing is that many people have a pretty low threshold for discomfort and pain. If you think about it, it isn't difficult to get through life without experiencing much pain and suffering. We have it pretty easy now compared to more brutal times.

We often hear nowadays about the sensitive 'snowflake' generation. The reference usually describes the ease with which they are offended, but it could easily be used to refer to physical prowess. Where once we toiled in the fields, the mines and the factories, automation has reduced the physical toll. Hands are now more used to a keyboard or smartphone screen than a pick axe or a pitchfork.

As it happens, I think humans need physicality. We need to sweat and toil. We need to feel physically exhausted. The problem with modern society is that we are all mentally shattered, but our bodies are largely unchallenged. We could describe the popularity of gyms, running and fitness in general, which is at an all-time high as people search for an alternative outlet for their physicality.

But even health and fitness can be smoke and mirrors in a society that places more importance on aesthetics than it does on substance. Social media and our vanity-obsessed society places more adulation on a rippling six-pack than it does on a solid pair of legs that can run for a couple of hours.

As a child, I was never sporty. In fact, I'd go so far as to say I hated it. A late learner, I can still remember a special swimming race that the school had to put on for me and another boy who couldn't swim. We had to *run* the width of the pool. Part of my hate of sport was a resignation to failure. I 'knew' that I wasn't going to do well, so I just sort of gave up.

It has taken me more than 25 years to learn the power of positive thinking. I like to think of myself as an optimist, but I haven't always been like that; on the contrary, I was a world-class pessimist. Pessimism breeds negativity and throughout my childhood I created a toxic attitude of failure. Failure was such a big part of my childhood. I failed in almost everything I turned my hand to.

I failed to stay at one school and ended up going to five different schools, and then to two different universities after dropping out of the first. I failed my exams. I failed to get into any teams. I failed my driving test seven times. I failed to get into drama school.

Failure loomed over me like a big black cloud. In retrospect, I could see that I was creating most of the gloom myself. My mind was set to negative. I had approached everything with the expectation of failure. The result was a fearful acceptance of failure that dogged me for years.

I'm not sure when or how I finally shook off the manacles of negativity. I'm not really sure when I stopped looking down and started looking up, but little by little that heavy dark cloud began to evaporate and was replaced by a bright sunbeam, and I think it was probably travel that really helped purge the pessimism. You see you can't really fail at travel. So much of life seems to be loaded to either success or failure, win or lose, pass or fail, in or out, but travel seemed to give me a fresh outlook. No one judged me, I was free to make my own path, there was no right and wrong.

I was 18 when I first travelled to South America alone. I travelled the length of the Brazilian Amazon on a cargo ship and then ended up teaching in the Ecuadorian Andes. The freedom and hope that came with travels through the unknown was heady and intoxicating. I found the whole experience enlightening. It sounds like a cliché, but I really did find myself.

Freed from the baggage of familiarity back at home, failure became a distant memory. From a world in which I had been 'tested' since I was seven years old, I felt like I had been released. It is probably why I still have such a problem with the modern education system. In the UK, we still place far too much pressure and expectation on exams. By relying on exam results to define a child, we are artificially inhibiting the growth of those who are no good under pressure. Exams are great for those who can cram information and then regurgitate it word for word. Indeed, there are plenty of jobs for which this skill is very useful.

It still surprises me how backwards or downwards looking our education system is. I often wonder why children are still being educated in the relatively clinical confines of a classroom when they could be learning in the outdoors. Plenty of other nations have adopted wilderness education successfully.

Now all of this is not to say that failure isn't necessary, indeed it is crucial to life. As Winston Churchill once said, 'If you haven't failed, then you haven't been trying hard enough.' Just like risk, it is pretty easy to mitigate failure, largely by taking the easy option.

At my school I remember being placed in a Maths class for those likely to fail their GCSEs. We were taught the basics to ensure a C grade. By doing so, we were relegating ourselves artificially.

I'm still not sure this was the best way to approach academia. When it is so loaded towards exam results, parents, schools, tutors and pupils will all work out how best to beat the system. When this happens, it simply becomes about ticking boxes and getting a single letter (A, B, C, D) that defines you.

Think about it. Isn't it incredible that you can take a human being, brimming with their own unique talents and abilities, and confine that person to a single letter? We love to categorise and place people within strata and the academic category is a very easy one to use. We place so much adulation on the ability to get an A grade in an exam. Now, without wanting to devalue that hard-earned grade, what good is that in the school of life?

Will an A grade help you find water or forage for food? Will it help you build a shelter? Will it help you communicate diplomatically with a tribe of people with whom you have no common language? Will it help you survive alone in an ocean? I'm not saying that we need all of these life skills, after all we have created a society in which we can avoid almost all of them, but is the mark of a great man or woman, the sum of their exam results? The answer is no. And yet society still obsesses about them. Your exam results will define your future.

Not only will they determine where and if you go to university or get a job or apprenticeship, but they also have the ability to shape your emotions. Take it from me, when you keep failing your exams, you descend into a perpetual cycle of negativity. It sucks you down into a vortex of pessimism, the 'cloud' grows and you instinctively become downward looking.

I'm not saying this is always the case. There are some strong-willed individuals who are able to show their brilliance through music, drama, art or sport. They are able to shield themselves from the shadow of the cloud by shining elsewhere.

But, for me, I can still remember the overwhelming feeling of gloom when I got my A level results: C, D, N. I couldn't see how I was ever going to shake 'failure'. I decided to place all my energy in drama. My mother was an actress. My best friend, Milly Fox, was already a successful actress in her own right. I had performed in a number of plays at school, one of which had even transferred to the Edinburgh Fringe Festival. Acting felt like something I was actually good at. It gave me confidence and happiness.

Then I got rejected by all 10 acting schools that I applied for.

They say 'what doesn't kill you makes you stronger', but I can tell you, those few months after the drama school rejections were pretty bleak. I couldn't see a way out. I felt like I was trapped in a hole: I could see the light above, but I couldn't reach it. All around was darkness. I touched depression. That will probably give you an insight into my fear of failure.

I am still deeply fearful of it, but my attitude and resilience have changed. The first time I really confronted my fear of failure proactively was when I signed up to run the Marathon des Sables, a 180-mile six-day race across the Sahara desert.

To this day, I'm not really sure where my decision came from. It certainly wasn't from any sane, level-headed place. I had never run in my life; maybe once, aged eight, at sports day but apart from that I had spent most of my life 'allergic' to sport. Why I suddenly thought I would be able to run 180 miles is beyond me. I suppose it was already evidence of my shift in attitude. I was beginning to look up rather than down.

Those six days remain some of the most uncomfortable and painful of my life, but the experience was profound. Somehow, I found the inner strength to overcome physical adversity.

I returned from the desert with a new resolve. The experience had strengthened me in unexpected ways. For the first time, I hadn't failed. I had completed the task. I hadn't done so in a record-breaking time and I hadn't done so with much elegance, but I had finished it. In some ways, the Marathon des Sables was an introduction to a world in which completing was just as important as competing.

Let's be honest, the world is such a competitive place that society naturally places a worth on hierarchy. In the animal kingdom, it is structured by strength. The alpha will always dominate. In society, I think we put a lot on our meritocracy. We like to believe someone has earned their position.

Sport is one of the arenas in which a combined show of strength, stamina and mental fortitude can separate one individual from another. Failure in sport depends on the athlete. James Cracknell used to describe anything but a gold medal as failure. For James, coming second was failure.

I suppose it's all relative. If I even reached the Olympic arena of sport, I would feel like I had won. To be chosen to represent your country would be enough, but when you have spent your life working towards a single goal, the line between success and failure becomes much more profound. I suppose you could argue that the lower you set your bar, the lower the chance of failure, but also the lower the sense of achievement.

Winston Churchill has a couple of more useful things to say on the subject: 'Success is going from failure to failure without a loss of enthusiasm' and 'A pessimist sees the difficulty in every opportunity; an optimist sees the opportunity in every difficulty.'

And of course, arguably his greatest rousing quote was: 'Never give in. Never give in. Never, never, never, never – in nothing, great or small, large or petty – never give in, except to convictions of honour and good sense.'

It is easy to sit here hypothesising about the spirit of human resilience and determination, but of course we all fail at some time. But, and I think this is the crucial point, we must fail because without failure there is no success. One necessitates the other. As much as I despise failure, I also recognise that it has played a crucial role in making me the person who I am.

Some of the most insufferable people I know have never failed. This breeds the arrogance of certainty. We need failure to make us more rounded, more humble. It's just that we don't want too much of it, or it creates a slightly broken spirit that spends the rest of their life trying to prove their self-worth through success wherever they can find it.

Sportsmen and women are of course the exception. They have been able to combine their unique physicality with the human need to perform. I think it's one of the reasons I have found myself drawn to them as expedition companions even despite my allergy to the sporting arena.

James Cracknell and I were complete strangers when we set off in our little rowing boat. I hoped that by partnering with James, not only was I teaming up with someone who could actually row a boat, but I was also going with someone who had the right mental aptitude: James had the competitive genes that I seemed to be missing. For someone fearful of failure, it was not only odd that I had teamed up with one of the most fiercely competitive and driven athletes in the world, but I had also joined a race across the Atlantic.

For some, rowing the Atlantic with a mate would be challenge enough, but I have always confronted my weakness face on. Accept it and work with your weakness, that's always been my mantra. Acknowledging it is the first step towards overcoming it.

Weakness is not synonymous with failure. Although there are many who will attribute all the negatives with failure, I happen to disagree. It's all about how you approach it and what you ultimately consider success.

Victoria and I both had an honest and philosophical approach to Everest. We went into the project with our eyes wide open. We both understood the risks, and after nearly two years of preparation, we also both knew the variables.

Unlike the professional sporting arena in which Olympic-level athletes are surrounded by a collaborative team of experts that focuses on everything from muscle tone and mental wellbeing to nutrition and even sleep, here in the mountains we would be on our own.

We had a world-class climber in Kenton Cool, but it was different to the sporting stage, and I suspect it was easier for me than Victoria who was more used to a small army of support staff than a few smiling sherpas. Victoria and I had talked at length about achievement, goals and what we wanted to get out of Everest. One of the main differences was our drive behind the climb. Mine was a childhood dream. Victoria's was more a post-competitive Olympian challenge.

Retirement can be pretty tough for all of us but particularly for athletes who have often passed their peak by the time they are 30. Where do you go after you have been the best in the world, competing at a professional level?

In the process of their intense training, many athletes have become institutionalised. They have been told when to wake, eat, sleep, and exercise all their lives. Their lives have been fully absorbed in their sporting excellence and then, suddenly, one day it is over. Like a food product that is past its sell by date, they find themselves discarded, often even before they are mouldy and when they are still perfectly fresh and ripe.

Victoria, to my mind, was dropped far too early. She is an astonishing sportswoman. Her drive and focus are extraordinary for someone who admits they never really enjoyed cycling that much. To have that kind of determination is remarkable and gives a revealing insight into her mental and physical aptitude.

She is also her own worst critic. I have never seen someone beat themselves up so much. It's like self-flagellation. Perhaps it was what drove her on to win her nine world titles and two Olympic golds, but it was also infuriating to be around.

We often climbed mountains in record time. We would all be euphoric with our experience, except for Victoria who would be criticising herself for the extra two minutes she spent stopping on the way up.

It was so inconsequential in the grand scheme of things, perhaps a couple of extra minutes in a 12-hour climb, but Victoria never let it go. It was like perpetual disappointment. However much Kenton and I tried to pull her up, she would drag herself down. I'd be lying if I said it didn't sometimes spill out to affect the team.

This constant performance loathing could be testing, but then that's what a team is about. It's about working with the collective strengths and weaknesses of the whole group.

Victoria brought far more to the expedition than she ever took away, but I sometimes found her Eeyore-like pessimism a little hard to take.

But one of the things that I will take away from this expedition was watching Victoria become more confident in the mountains. I loved seeing it. Our friendship was formed through low-impact attrition. Victoria, Kenton and I spent a lot of time together in some pretty testing environments.

We had been on such an incredible journey together. So, to have seen Victoria suffering as she was at Camp 2, was awful. The severity of the situation was obvious.

We were all worried about her. We knew that it would be foolish to continue, but who were we to tell her that? As a team of course, we had a responsibility to look out for each other, but to tell another teammate that they couldn't go on felt wrong. We could advise her and arm her with the information she needed to make her own educated and informed decision, but I didn't think we had the right to tell her she needed to quit.

Victoria had confided to us the fact that she was fed up of people telling her she could and couldn't do something. For so much of her life, she had been told that she would be unable to do things by other people. Indeed, it was her coach who (in my mind, unfairly) told her she wouldn't have the physical or mental capabilities to compete in a third Olympics and so bypassed her for another cyclist – a decision that had left her so enraged and angered.

Who can blame her? No one likes to be told what you can and can't do. The proof is in the pudding. Let the results speak for themselves. Part of the attraction of the expedition for Victoria was that she could sink or swim on her own ability and results. She was beholden to no one. She wasn't on Everest to win a gold medal but to try and exorcise the demons of those who have always told her what she can't do rather than what she can do.

Our whole philosophy revolved around a can-do attitude. My dear friend Haya Bint Al Hussein, who helped enable the expedition, had created a foundation, the Anything is Possible movement, centred entirely on this philosophy. Victoria had more strength and drive than any of us. On the face of it, I always felt she had more of a chance to reach the summit than me, but it was her physiology that was letting her down.

I lay in my tent, tormented by the complexity of our situation. On the one hand, we were a team driven by our goal to summit together. We wanted to achieve our dreams and inspire others to fulfil their own ambitions. Freed from the shackles of management, expectations, trainers and funding, Victoria was trying to pursue a simpler, unadulterated dream.

On the other hand, she had just nearly died. Not through an avalanche but through the unstoppable misfortune of altitude sickness which has the ability to strike like lightning. By continuing, we all knew that she would not only be risking her own life, but also those around her who would be more vulnerable if she fell ill again and needed rescuing. Not only would it effectively put lives at risk, but it would jeopardise the chances of a successful summit. Our focus would be on Vic's welfare more than the overall objective.

We were stuck almost literally between a rock and a hard place and none of us was sure where to turn.

It's incredible how quickly humans can bounce back from the deadly effects of altitude sickness. The only sure way of treating it is to descend until the symptoms desist. At Base Camp, there was an instantaneous recovery. Looking at Victoria, it was hard to believe that just a couple of hours before she had been knocking at death's door.

Everest ER was our first port of call. Situated in the middle of Base Camp, the temporary hospital is run on a charitable basis by volunteer doctors from across the world. For 30 minutes, we traversed Base Camp until we reached the large white tent. At the entrance was a large sign advertising various high-altitude medicines for sale. At the top of the list, I was surprised to see Viagra – apparently it has increasingly become the drug of choice for mountaineers because it actually increases blood flow everywhere in the body.

Victoria disappeared into the consultation room while I paced up and down outside. I felt my Everest dream slipping from my grasp. We had thankfully avoided a greater tragedy but carrying on felt churlish. If Victoria decided to end her bid, then so would I. We were a team. It felt wrong to carry on without her.

I knew that the doctor would make the decision for her. Her statistics on the mountain had been life threatening. Any medic would realise the risks. Fifteen minutes later, she emerged from the tent with a couple of Paracetamol and the encouragement to carry on. I'd be lying if I didn't say I was surprised. I was no medic and the mountains were still a new environment to me, but I understood enough of the basics to read the risks. Altitude sickness had nearly killed her the first time. Going up again felt like suicide.

On the walk back to camp, I voiced my concerns. Victoria still had no comprehension of just how vulnerable she had been. I reiterated to her how worried we had been and stopped short of telling her to quit.

It was an impossible situation.

Back in London, we had been working with Sundeep Dhillon, a two-time summiting doctor who had been a part of the Xtreme Everest expedition in which a team of doctors had ascended Everest with a full medical laboratory, taking VO2 max tests, blood and even muscle biopsy along the route.

Sundeep is an unassuming man of remarkable achievements. He had tested our physiology before we left, and he already knew and understood Victoria's weaknesses when it came to altitude.

Victoria decided to call him for a second opinion. She spoke to Sundeep at length before talking to Kenton and as many other referrals as she could. She needed to arm herself with as much information as possible, before she could make her own informed decision.

A couple of hours later, I joined her on the hill overlooking Base Camp. We sat on a pile of rubble and stared at the Khumbu Icefall ahead of us.

'I've decided not to go on,' she explained calmly.

Tears streamed down my cheeks as she explained her decision to put life ahead of ambition.

'I used to feel like a superhero, but for the first time in my life I feel my body has let me down,' she sobbed.

It was heart-breaking. Although I knew it was the correct, sensible decision to make, it was hard to hear its reality. Victoria and I were a team. The team. We had started this together and we would finish this together, or not, as it turned out.

'Then I'm not going to carry on. We're in this together,' I added, wiping the tears from my eyes.

'I want you to carry on. This is more your dream than mine. It's always been your dream, and I want you to continue. Do it for me, Ben,' she smiled.

To be honest, I felt a bit of a failure myself. I had wanted us to achieve this together. We had formed an unlikely duo, but this had always been a partnership. We each brought something unique and different to the team dynamic. Victoria had always been there. She was an integral part of the Everest dream. To continue without her felt like losing a limb, an asset, a part of our Everest DNA. To have to go our separate ways now, so early in the expedition, was as painful as it was disappointing.

Once again, the contradictions were overwhelming. Relief that she and she alone had made the very sensible decision to cut her losses and quit while she was ahead, but the bitter disappointment that we wouldn't continue this adventure together.

From the very start, we had always been clear that the journey was the destination. The whole adventure was the adventure. Summiting would be the bonus. We both wanted to enjoy the process. The years of planning, the months of cold and suffering. The deprivations and the rationing, the beauty and the magnificence. The travel, teamwork and the adventure. We had both made a commitment to make the most of this process, irrespective of the outcome. Of course, I'd be lying if I said that the ultimate goal of standing atop the world didn't haunt my thoughts. It taunted me and tantalised me. It was as terrifying as it was intoxicating.

And now, here, on this little pile of rubble at Base Camp, our collective dream had disappeared. Our shattered hopes of standing on the summit together swirled around us as we sat in silence, digesting the magnitude of the decision.

I felt flat as I walked to my tent.

Victoria hadn't decided if she wanted to stay on at Base Camp. Sundeep had warned us to think about such a scenario. 'Some people choose to stay on,' he had explained, 'to support the team effort, while others want to head home.'

For many, the painful constant reminder of what they had sacrificed becomes too much. In a way, I wanted Victoria to stay. Perhaps it was for selfish reasons. I like consistency and always fear change. I think it's perhaps a symptom of my nomadic life, that I cling onto anything habitual. I like routine. I like familiarity. When I'm home, which isn't often, I will often find myself sticking rigidly to a routine each day. It is grounding. I think it's a symptom of a life of change. I'm a keen advocate that variety is the spice of life, but sometimes routine can be just as effectual.

After a couple of days back at Base Camp, Victoria decided to leave. As disappointed as I was, I couldn't blame her. Family matters and the bitter disappointment of her decision didn't make Base Camp a particularly pleasant place to languish.

Base Camp is fit for purpose. A perfect place for the dreaming romantics, still hopeful for an ascent, but a pretty bleak, soulless place for those who have stepped back from their summit aspirations. Within a couple of hours of her decision, she was on a helicopter back to Kathmandu. We hugged at the rough heliport built from rubble atop the glacier.

And with that, she was gone.

Empty. Listless. Lost.

Disappointment was tempered by the relief that she was now on her way back to good health and fitness, but also the hollow feeling that I had lost my teammate and friend.

The climb had been well-documented in the UK and I also knew she was heading back into the media lion's den. I hoped the press would be kind to her. Hers was not failure. It was just a different ending.

CHAPTER TEN

POSITIVITY

Boom!

The sonic power from the explosion was louder and more ferocious than any other avalanche I had heard. There followed a panic of torch light that reflected off my tent.

I lay there frozen in my sleeping bag in the relative security of Base Camp, my mind once again running riot. I wondered where the avalanche had hit and if it had taken out the icefall. This one sounded larger than any other I had heard. My hairs stood on end as goose bumps formed on my arms.

Slowly, I drifted back to sleep.

BOOM!

This one was even louder. My whole body shook. It sounded like it was on top of me. I flinched and prepared myself for impact. Surely this time the avalanche would hit us.

There followed a light so bright that it lit up my whole tent. Was it a helicopter? The wind was snapping at the tent. I struggled to comprehend what was going on. There must have been at least two violent avalanches and I could see my tent billowing from the weight of snow that had built up.

I lay there. Heart racing.

BOOM!! This time it was almost deafening. In my sleepy, oxygen-starved state, I simply couldn't work out what was happening. Again, a flash of light illuminated the whole tent, but this time it was blindingly bright.

'What the hell?'

I pulled on my down jacket and crawled towards the door flap of the tent to peer outside. As I unzipped it, I could make out a flurry of snow. Then *BOOM!!* followed by an almighty flash.

A violent storm was almost on top of us. I had never heard or experienced thunder and lightning like it. And the wind was howling. Perhaps it was our elevation. Maybe it was the intensity and ferocity of the storm, but it was like stepping inside the storm itself.

I stared up at the Khumbu Icefall. In the darkness, I could just about make out a couple of headlamps of climbers in the midst of the icefall. Then a sudden burst of lightning illuminated every crag and crevasse as if it was daylight. It was like watching a horror film. I pitied anyone in that terrible place right now. I withdrew back into my tent, pulled my sleeping bag tightly over me and prayed that a stray fork of lightning wouldn't hit our high, exposed tents.

In the morning, I emerged to a winter wonderland. Nearly a foot of snow had carpeted Base Camp. It looked like a different world. It was actually a little more inviting. More like a winter ski resort now, only with tents and prayer flags.

I trudged down to the mess tent. Everyone was talking about the mighty storm. Kenton, in all his years on Everest, had never experienced anything like it. More incredible still was the fact that in the midst of nature's wrath, Ant and Ed had headed out for their final summit rotation.

Kenton had been wrestling with dates and scenarios. The mountain was still not completely roped. The sherpas who were up at Camp 4 still had to rope the final 800 metres, a mighty section of mountain that they hoped to have done by the following day if the weather improved.

The problem was that the weather wasn't improving and it wasn't predicted to do so. A quick glance at Camp 1 revealed angry swirls of snow being blown into vast licks by the 100 mph winds. With these conditions at 6,000 metres, the camps higher up would be even more inhospitable. But some good weather was approaching and the key to Kenton's decision making was ensuring that we were in the right place at the right time. Get it wrong and at best we would fail to summit, and at worst we would die.

Making a call on the final rotation is what separates the wheat from the chaff and one of the reasons for having Kenton as guide was his ability to call it successfully. We had pushed for an early summit and I had broached the subject of departing the night before, when Ant and Ed had left.

The presence of another film crew had put pressure on me. I felt an extra burden. There was competition. Although we were all in it together, I felt I needed to keep up with Ant. The humiliation of being out-summited was something I dreaded.

It wasn't to do with speed or haste. Funnily enough, it was more like queuing up for the checkout in a supermarket, I wanted to ensure I was in the right queue. I didn't want to be watching as others advanced more quickly in their line.

The sherpas implored us to wait for a day. Their colleagues up at Camp 4 were struggling to fix the mountain and that the untimely arrival of Western climbers would add an unnecessary burden to their already hazardous work. Knowing that Ant and Ed were heading off added to my confusion. If they were doing it, then why weren't we? After all, I was with a master summiteer. But that meant I had to trust him. Kenton explained that the high winds would make Camp 2 and above intolerable. There were already reports of tents being blown away up there.

It seemed a sensible decision, but still Ant and Ed's stealing a march on us, troubled me. I looked up at the swirling angry wind that was whipping tails of snow off the higher peaks. I hadn't seen the mountain like this since we had arrived. She looked angry. Like she was asserting her authority and power.

I have always had a great respect for nature. The wilderness has a tremendous power that mankind naively thinks it can overcome. You only have to look at the devastation caused by tsunamis, floods, earthquakes and volcanoes to be reminded that we will always be overpowered.

I spent the day preparing for our departure the following morning, once the winds had died down sufficiently. It would be our summit bid. I made a note to myself: 'Summarise how many rotations you had completed and how much preparation you had done (training). Useful to take stock before you head up.'

We were coming up to our final summit rotation – and I mean *the final* rotation. This time we would be leaving Base Camp in a boom or bust attempt on the summit of Mount Everest.

And our choice of film in camp before our final summit rotation?

Have you ever rewatched the classic *Ferris Bueller's Day Off*, in which Ferris, a high-school senior, fakes being sick one day, in order to skip school with two friends for an adventure in downtown Chicago in his dad's Ferrari? If not, I implore you to avoid it. It first came out more than 30 years ago, and had once been my favourite movie, but unfortunately it hasn't dated well.

I retired to my tent before the film was over and lay there listening to the sounds of the synthesised 'sick machine' from the movie floating across from the mess tent. The camp was still being buffeted by the wind that had gripped the mountain. The sherpas had fixed all but the very final section of climb and we were ready for our bid.

I lay in my tent in a dazed stupor. This was it. My one and only chance. While some people return time and time again, I knew that Marina's strength and generosity would only stretch to the one attempt.

If I failed to reach the summit, I had promised myself to come back with a smile on my face and the resolution that I had given it my best and would lay to rest my summit dream. It wasn't an unreasonable settlement.

I wanted to summit Everest so badly. It haunted my dreams and dominated my thoughts, and yet I always tried to remind myself that its outcome was fraught with variables, many of which were out of my control. Apart from illness, altitude sickness or an accident, there was the chance of a lost piece of kit. One lost glove, blown away in the wind, can spell disaster. And that's not just my glove; any one of the team's gloves going astray and we would all be returning to Base Camp. Environmental and geological disasters were an ever-present risk too, as the previous few days had amply shown: earthquakes, storms, catastrophic ice collapses and avalanches had closed the whole mountain in previous years. Other human factors like strikes by sherpas, and dying climbers, would also put paid to any summit bid. As would bureaucratic problems: revoked licences and even the Nepalese authorities closing the mountain at the eleventh hour could all thwart us.

It is these variables that make any attempt to summit Everest so vulnerable and volatile. There are a multitude of factors that have to work in your favour before you can even begin. Just as the 100-metre sprinter spends four hard years before he or she even reaches the start line at the Olympics, so we had worked tirelessly and cleared a number of hurdles just to get to the starting point of our journey.

Under moonlight, we gathered outside the mess tent and once again performed our little Puja ceremony. The juniper was already burning in the little fire for Ant and Ed, and I was relieved that they placed another small pile among the flames for us. I picked up a couple of handfuls of rice and threw them towards the mountain before putting a few grains in my pocket for good measure.

Then we began the long trek up towards the Pinnacles, back up through the by now familiar, but always scary Khumbu Icefall. Within seven hours we made it to Camp 2. Shattered and exhausted, I collapsed on the little tent's floor. Ant and Ed had been holed up here by the powerful winds that had damaged much of the camp, as tents had been stripped and blown away. Kit had been lost and scattered across the valley. Some climbers had watched in horror as their dreams were blown away in front of their very eyes. Many were forced to retreat down the mountain without gear, heading home with their hopes in tatters.

Ed and Ant had climbed through the biblical electric storm and endured such powerful winds that they had been forced to retreat into a tent at Camp 1 until the winds abated slightly. I wondered why they hadn't simply deferred their summit bid by a day to climb in better, safer conditions. After all, we were now all in the same place, ready for a perfect summit bid in just two days.

The winds still howled and swirled high above us. A conical grey cloud clung to the summit in an otherworldly vision of menace – a necromancer's cap. Within that cloud was a whirling vortex of hurricane-force winds, the likes of which had killed better mountaineers than us.

Camp 2 was still being buffeted but there was word from the meteorological office that the winds would abate within 12 hours. We would need to acclimatise at Camp 2 for at least another 24 hours before heading higher, to stand any chance of reaching the summit.

Having already spent a day holed up at Camp 2, Ant and Ed decided to soldier on into the eye of the storm. By the time we awoke early the next day, they had gone.

The wind snapped at our tent all day. The predicted break in the weather hadn't come, but Kenton was sure that things would improve by the time we set off for Camp 3 the following morning. While most people don't use oxygen until above 7,000 metres at

Camp 3, Kenton suggested I use some supplementary oxygen to help me with my fear of the Lhotse Face. I declined the early oxygen. I wanted to embrace and feel the mountain unaided.

Although I had been up to Camp 3 before, the wall still horrified me. I had only ascended a short part of it previously. I knew that I had a further two-thirds of the wall to climb before I even reached the Geneva Spur and Yellow Band ahead of Camp 4 at 8,000 metres. The ascent to Camp 3 was tougher than I remembered. Five weeks on the mountain had taken its toll. I had lost muscle mass from my whole body, but it was my legs in particular that burned with the exertion.

I felt like my energy had been blown away with the wind. The steep wall of ice meant there was nowhere to stop and rest. The most I could do was rest my knees and scrunch up my eyes in pain.

We finally reached Camp 3 and I clambered into the tent with Sherpa Ang Thindu. Broken and exhausted, I could barely think. I lay in the tent as the little stove burned brightly, melting the snow and ice.

Before starting the climb, I had spent 10 days on a remote island in the Arctic Circle with Randi Skaug, a Norwegian explorer and veteran of Everest. 'Smile,' had been Randi's advice to me before I left. 'Don't let the mountain strip you of your smile.'

A broad grin broke across my face. I was here. I was at Camp 3 on my final bid to reach the summit. The smile flooded me with happiness and confidence. I felt a wave of contentment. Gone was the exhaustion and the fear, the worry and the anxiety.

I was here. I was *really* here, looking out of the little tent, perched precariously on a ledge cut into the icy slope. I had made it this far. 'Look Up,' I heard a voice in my head. The heavy, menacing clouds had started to clear. A gap had appeared through which the sun projected long tentacles of light, through which the wind-blown snow was illuminated like confetti. It was so beautiful and ethereal. I felt a sense of belonging. They say that mountains have a way of capturing your soul and spirit, that once you are within their bosom you will be forever lost within their towering snowy peaks. I felt such a deep connection. It was like a peaceful resolution, like a battle had ended in a truce. I wasn't there yet, but it felt empowering nonetheless.

The wind gradually disappeared overnight so that in the morning all was still. Under a bright sun, I connected my oxygen mask and bottle for the first time and we began the slow climb up the upper section of the Lhotse Face. The slope became steeper and more exposed as we reached the higher flanks.

By now, angry clouds had once again started to gather in the skies above us. Powerful gusts of wind streamed across the slopes threatening to blow us off the mountain. A couple of teams had already begun to retreat, but Kenton suggested we hold our nerve and carry on towards Camp 4. We were already more than halfway and returning through the gathering storm would be even more hazardous; the best solution was to carry on upwards in the hope that the promised clear weather would finally arrive.

I had been looking forward to crossing the Geneva Spur, which had sounded so much easier and less scary than the steep climb up the Lhotse Face. How wrong I was. The traverse was agonisingly difficult. With the fresh snow, it was impossible to get a good step in. The result was that I slipped several feet every other

step. It slowed me down even more and the biting wind was gathering in speed.

The wind chill was now minus 25 °C. Kenton had warned me
to cover up the little area of skin left unprotected between my
oxygen mask and goggles, but I had failed to do so, and now I
could feel the wind stinging the exposed skin. Head down, I
battled on into the raging storm. Visibility was down to just 20
metres and at times it felt like walking in a snow globe. White.
White. White. I began to feel alone and vulnerable for the first
time.

We were heading up to 8,000 metres, well into the death zone
where you very quickly mentally and physically decline towards
death, which is why it is the stage for so many losses of life, tragedies and disasters on the mountain. I wondered whether Kenton
had made the right call. So many other teams with much better
climbers than myself had already turned back and yet we were
soldiering on. At that altitude, the air pressure is about a third of
that at sea-level. Everything becomes strenuous, exhausting.

I started to worry about Ant and Ed. We knew that they had
made a summit bid the previous evening. The winds higher up
the mountain would be even more intense. It was already noon.
If they had successfully summited, then they would be well on
their way down heading towards Camp 3. If they were on sched-
ule, they really should pass us at some point before we reached
Camp 4.

Onwards we climbed in the powerful wintry conditions of the
blizzard. Occasionally, I would be blown off my feet as I struggled
to maintain my balance. The final spur before Camp 4 involved a
difficult climb up a narrow rocky face. Even in the limited

visibility, its exposure to the long drop below was scary. My vertigo began to resurface as I struggled to haul myself up the icy, wind-buffeted face.

It seemed to take an eternity before I finally emerged onto a moonlike landscape of rubble and boulders. It was just a short walk to Camp 4 from here along a comparatively flat route, but like everything on Everest, nothing is easy. Hurricane-force winds now ripped across the plateau.

'It's too windy to put any tents up,' hollered Kenton over the deafening din of the wind as we approached camp. Camp 4, which is also known as the South Col, is arguably as famous as the mountain itself. It has been the scene of so many Everest tales. At 8,000 metres, it is, to be honest, a pretty wretched place. The ground was littered with destroyed and tattered tents, their pegs and poles protruding from the snow and ice like the stripped trees after a tornado. A dozen tents sat among the detritus and the remains of previous expeditions that were strewn across the site.

In my exhaustion and oxygen-deprived mind, it was difficult to make out what I was seeing. I couldn't tell if this had been a fully functioning, bustling camp that had been destroyed overnight, or whether this was the build-up of discarded kit from 65 years of summit attempts. I stepped over enamel mugs and plates; there were stoves and spoons, old boots and chocolate bars still in their wrappers. Most of it looked fresh. I could have picked up the packets of noodles and tins of food and eaten them.

I bent my body into the gusting wind. I was desperate to lie down. Over the din of the wind, I spotted a familiar face. It was Ed, Ant's cameraman. He looked beaten. His face was weathered and gaunt. I was shocked at how thin and pale he looked. I took off my pack and oxygen mask and slowly wandered over to him to congratulate them on their summit.

He looked at me. There was nothing behind his eyes. It was like he was looking through me. I went to give him a hug and he collapsed against my shoulders, his body shaking violently while he sobbed uncontrollably. 'We can't find Ant, he's somewhere on the mountain.'

My stomach lurched. It was 4 pm. They had summited at 7 am and Ed had last seen Ant an hour later before they became separated. Ed had already been back at Camp 4 for nearly four hours. It didn't add up. I struggled to comprehend what I was hearing. Ant, the Special Forces super-hero, was missing on the mountain and the weather was worsening.

A huge dark, ominous cloud had built up to the east of the mountain. The sky looked menacing and angry. My breathing became short. I needed oxygen. I slowly walked to my rucksack and sat next to it in the ice amid the wreckage of previous expeditions. It looked like an airplane had crashed and its contents had been strewn across the ice field.

I pulled the mask to my face and tried to compute what was happening. We couldn't put up a tent, the storm was worsening, and Ant was missing. It was like stepping into my worst Everest nightmare. I thought back to all the unfolding tragedies that had happened here on this very spot, and now I was in the midst of my own.

I sat there. Dazed. Numb. The wind was building again. We had no shelter and I didn't have the strength to descend. Even if we did, I knew it would take many hours to get back down to

Camp 3 which wouldn't do us much good anyway. We were at a crossroads and didn't know where any of the roads ended. I was cold, hungry, tired and thirsty, but all I could think about was Ant. Missing. Somewhere on the summit of Everest. What had happened? I had seen both Ant and Ed climbing together. They were equally matched. In some ways, they were the perfect partnership. Ed's superior climbing was slightly handicapped by the burden of his camera, which meant he and Ant had an equal pace.

I could understand a 30-minute difference in their descent times, but four hours seemed incomprehensible. In my numb stupor, Kenton and the sherpas had battled against the wind to erect one of the tents. Ed, Kenton and I clambered inside. The fabric of the door flap snapped violently in the ever-increasing wind.

I lay in the tent and sobbed. I had never in my life felt so helpless and vulnerable. Suddenly, the threat of Everest seemed very real. I felt a surge of panic as I watched the sides of the tent warp alarmingly. I had seen tents withstand some pretty major storms, but never on an exposed col at 8,000 metres. One tiny tear in the tent fabric and the wind would rip it to shreds. One loose guy-line or one sun-damaged section of the tent and it could be stripped from its poles like the dozens of other tents that littered the camp.

I peered out at the looming black cloud. My mind went as dark and foggy as the horizon. My breathing became short. I grabbed my mask again and took a few deep breaths.

'Pull yourself together,' I berated myself. I had to control my mind which was beginning to wander. I was losing control. Panic was welling up at the wretchedness of the situation.

I looked at Mark and Kenton. They were both staring up at the top of the tent. Violent gusts of wind were pressing the tent down towards our faces, the pressure bowing the poles. If I hadn't had the experience of life-threatening storms in Antarctica, I would have convinced myself that the tents couldn't possibly withstand such a battering.

How had Ed and Ant separated? Did they mean to split up? Where was Ant? Was he with a sherpa? I had so many questions. I could hear Ed's voice booming over the sound of the wind as he zipped down our tent and crouched down, his face crusted in ice.

He explained that Ant was with two sherpas, and that although they all had radios he couldn't get through to any of them. Kenton jumped to attention and became very methodical. He pulled out the booster antenna and attached it to our radio. 'Kenton to Ant, Kenton to Ant, do you copy?' He repeated it several times. 'Kenton to Ant, if you can hear this, press your button once.' Still no reply.

Garrett Madison was way down the mountain at Camp 2 with his climbing group, but he was already aware of a problem on the summit. His voice crackled over the radio. 'Can you confirm if everyone is back at Camp 4, over?'

'Ant and two sherpas, total three persons, are unaccounted for, over,' replied Kenton.

There was a short pause. 'To confirm, Ant and two sherpas are at Camp 4, that's great news, over.'

'No, Ant and two sherpas are still on the mountain. I repeat, Ant and two sherpas are *not* at Camp 4, over.'

The words hung around like a bad smell. Tears welled up in my eyes again as reality began to set in. They had now been missing for almost eight hours.

'It was chaos up there,' explained Ed. 'I saw a sherpa fall off the cornice, there was a Chinese girl, eyes wide like a f***ing rabbit, unable to move.'

'A sherpa fall off the cornice,' I repeated in my head, 'a sherpa fall off the cornice.' It took a while for me to comprehend what he was telling me. To fall off the cornice surely meant death. Had people died up there?

I buried my face in my sleeping bag. This was a living nightmare. What had gone wrong? Where had this storm come from? We had been assured of relatively benign weather in the forecast. Of course, there had been plenty of times when weather forecasts were wrong in the past, but things had changed. Everest weather prediction is now big business. Climbers rely on it for their ascents.

But here we were riding out a massive storm in the death zone with what now sounded like 10 climbers missing and presumed dead on the mountain. I felt sick. What had happened to them? Were they lost? Had they slipped? My imagination ran wild once again as images from the many tragic Everest stories raced through my mind. I pictured those climbers from that ill-fated 1996 expedition in their huddle just a short distance from Camp 4. So close and yet so far.

Marina – Summit fever

While risk can be calculated for the expedition overall, my biggest fear was that Ben might succumb to something called 'summit fever'. Infamous in the mountaineering world, summit fever is when climbers are consumed by a mad, all-consuming desire to keep on going regardless of whether that quest will end in death. Peter Hillary, son of Edmund Hillary, described seeing this in the British climber, Alison Hargreaves while climbing K2, Everest's slightly smaller but even more deadly sister, in 1995. In the final push, Hillary had noticed sinister weather fronts building as darkness was falling and made the seemingly obvious decision to return to camp while Hargreaves and her team made the disastrous decision to continue. 'They had all become blinkered by the summit. They had become obsessed by that, but I had become obsessed by the huge cloud banks that were building in the north.' Hargreaves and seven other climbers perished that night in the storm that they could all clearly see building.

Summit fever was what killed Rob Hall, whose death from exposure on the south summit of Everest in 1996 was one of the stories that haunted me while Ben was climbing. He'd insisted that his great friend and client, Doug Hansen continue to the summit rather than turn around and admit defeat, in spite of storm clouds brewing and the fact that it was far later in the day than was safe. This was Hansen's final attempt; he'd given everything to Everest, all his money and all his energy. If he didn't make it up this time, he never would. No one can understand Rob's reasoning, it was uncharacteristic of his great and much-admired expertise. His reputation belied his sense and was built on making decisions that were often tough to make but ended up being the right ones.

Ben had promised me that he wouldn't succumb to summit fever; he had too much to lose, he insisted. But then so did Rob. The transcripts of his final phone call to his heavily pregnant wife, as he lay dying on the side of the mountain he knew so well, still bring tears to my eyes, with his final words, 'Don't worry about me, I'm fine.'

I kept on telling myself that Ben was too sensible to let anything like this happen. It was this I clutched to as I thought of him high up on that perilous mountain.

But in the dark days, when I didn't know where he was and why it was taking so long, my mind played cruel tricks. In spite of his resolve, I had a creeping unease that summit fever was a lot easier to succumb to than I'd initially thought. Hot on the heels of Ant Middleton, a film crew in tow, the Daily Telegraph *poised to publish a summit shot and 150,000 Instagram followers waiting with bated breath, I realised with horror that turning around, admitting defeat, however obvious the decision, would be nigh on impossible.*

I peered out of the tent again. The wind was raging, whipping up the thin layer of snow cover. The angry cloud now enveloped the top of the mountain. We could see the route ahead, marked with a single rope on a near-vertical white slope. There was no sign of any climbers as far as the eye could see. There were just a few hours of daylight left.

I sat in the tent with my face buried in my sleeping bag. My oxygen mask strapped to my face. The tent snapped in the ever-increasing wind as we waited for news from the mountain.

We took turns to peer out of the tent onto the mountain slope. Nothing.

It's strange where the mind turns to in the hours of darkness.

I felt loss. Fear. Loathing.

I looked at my children's names that I had scrawled onto my sleeves in indelible marker as a reminder of what I had left behind. I grasped my wedding ring that was on a chain around my neck to avoid cutting off circulation in my swollen fingers. I longed for home and my loved ones.

I imagined the pain of talking to Ant's wife and family and telling them how much he had enjoyed his last few weeks on the mountain. I lay there and wept. I wept for Ant. I wept for the wretchedness of the moment and I wept for my lost dream.

People were missing on the mountain. My summit bid was over, I was convinced of that, and our priority was to find our missing friends. But the mountain was angry, furious and we were in the death zone, caught in the eye of the storm.

I peered out of the tent. A jet-black cloud the colour of tar was looming from the Tibetan side of the mountain. We were stuck in hurricane-force winds in the death zone with half a dozen missing climbers and sherpas. If I had concocted a nightmare before we set off, it would have looked like this.

We lay there for what felt like an interminable amount of time. Ed went to check the radio traffic again. There was still no news from the mountain.

Then Kenton took another look outside. In the distance, he spotted something.

'I think I have a visual.'

'One, two, three, four, five … six.'

'I have a visual on six climbers!'

He grabbed the radio and immediately messaged the team at Base Camp and Camp 2. As they got closer and closer, we could make out the familiar beard of Ant. The relief was unbelievable. Kenton burst into tears too. The combination of altitude, exhaustion, worry, fear and stress had worn us all down. We lay there in shock. Their final journey was over; for us, it was just the beginning.

Through that night, the three of us lay there in that tent as the wind howled with a violence and anger I had rarely heard before. The pressure would sometimes compress the whole tent so that it squashed across our faces and somehow, snow and ice blasted in through the zipped-up flaps covering us with a dusting of snow. I pulled my oxygen mask on and off for those next few hours, in an effort to conserve oxygen. We would now be forced to spend an extra day in the death zone with only limited oxygen.

It was hard to believe the tents could withstand this kind of battering. It wouldn't take much to shred them. One little tear or hole and the material would be stripped from above us, exposing us to the violence of the wind and ice. Without the protection of the tent we wouldn't survive for long out here. It was the longest night of my life.

By morning the wind had abated. We stepped out from our little yellow tent into a sea of destruction. Bags and kit had been blown across the already wind-torn, weather-wrecked camp. It was difficult to tell what was old and what was new damage as we wandered through the wreckage in shock, like survivors from an air crash.

Ant was not in a good way after his descent. Without sunglasses, he found the reflection from the intense sunlight on the snow and ice had temporarily blinded him. Weathered and beaten, he and Ed began their descent back to Base Camp, while we gathered ourselves and prepared for our final bid for the summit.

Emotionally and physically drained, I pulled myself together. I had to silence the inner doubt. I was in the death zone. So close and yet so far. I had never in my life been so isolated and remote from the outside world. If we perished now, our bodies would be left where they lay.

The feeling of utter isolation and solitude was both liberating and terrifying.

I felt so vulnerable.

The only way was Up.

CHAPTER ELEVEN

ADVERSITY

We all face adversity at some point in our lives. It can strike like lightning. We can never prepare ourselves for all eventualities, but we can arm ourselves to cope better.

For me, part of the attraction of expeditions and heading out into the wilderness is to take myself out of my comfort zone and give me perspective. Without experience of adversity, we are ill-prepared to cope with the unexpected.

Life is full of ups and downs. It's this contrast that makes it so interesting. Can you imagine how dull it would be if it was always consistent? We might avoid pain, suffering and unhappiness, but without ever experiencing those sentiments we would be equally unable to experience euphoria, happiness and ecstasy. It's the light and shade that brings texture and meaning to our lives.

Inevitably in life, we will all suffer the pain of loss. Losing someone we love must be one of the most painful experiences we have to go through, but for me it was the pain of losing someone I never got to know that shook me to my core.

I was filming for NBC News in Russia when Marina sent me a photograph of a positive pregnancy test. The little cross marked another chapter in our lives. We already had two children, but we had both dreamed of a third. We both came from families of three siblings and I think we instinctively always wanted to replicate what we had.

It wasn't to be. Willem's death crushed us. Marina remained in hospital while I looked after the children in a beautiful house overlooking Salzburg. We had to arrange for our stillborn son to be cremated and for his ashes to be sent home.

Two weeks after losing little Willem, Marina was discharged from hospital and we all flew home. It was a particularly poignant flight. We had flown out with the hopes and dreams of a family that was soon to be five, and returned empty and hollow, a family of four. Her stomach was still distended from the pregnancy and the trauma, and a young girl sitting next to Marina on the flight asked when she was due.

It's strange how we cope with adversity. I held it together pretty well. My focus was all directed at Ludo, Iona and Marina. I put them first. Everything was about them. In hindsight, I probably should have focused a little on my own mental anguish, but I was so preoccupied with trying to regain control of our life.

Marina grieved openly. She would often weep uncontrollably while I held her tightly. My own grieving was internal. I found it difficult to digest. I was grieving for someone I had never met. I gave up work for a month and stayed with my family, but life goes on and eventually I returned to work. It sounds strange, but I felt a strong sense of guilt. Guilt that something so monumental had happened, and yet I was returning to normality.

As the months went on, I found myself becoming increasingly insular. I began to have panic attacks in public places. I can remember going to an awards ceremony on my own, as I had done dozens if not hundreds of times before, but this time, I found myself hiding in the loo, suffering social anxiety. I eventually fled in tears. This wasn't me. I felt I was losing control. And therein was the problem.

In losing Willem, I had lost control of the one thing I have always been able to do: protect my family. Instead, I had been thousands of miles away. I was powerless and helpless.

I found myself becoming more and more reclusive. Eventually, I sought help. We had been seeing a counsellor to help us through the grieving process and she was able to help me understand why I was feeling as I was. It was a strange feeling of vulnerability that I hadn't experienced since childhood. It was like my confidence had taken a kicking. All my hard work to boost my self-esteem over the years had been lost and I needed a way to recapture it.

The reason I am such an advocate of taking risks is precisely because adversity will strike each of us at least some point in our lives. Without risk taking, we simply don't have the mental aptitude to cope when the shit really hits the fan. Rather naively, I assumed that Everest would be a breeze; after all I had rowed the Atlantic and walked to the South Pole. Many more people had climbed Everest. How hard could it be?

But Willem loomed large on Everest.

Perhaps it was the spirituality of the place. Perhaps it was the fact that he was the catalyst. Maybe it's because I missed him, but I felt his presence often.

The first time was on my way to Camp 3. I was on my second rotation and quite frankly it was terrifying. I felt helplessly out of my comfort zone. The Lhotse Face was icy and hot. The sheer wall confounded me. As I dug my crampons into the blue ice, I asked myself why I was there. It was a mountain wobble, but this one felt more significant.

As the thin mountain air stole my breath, I stared deep into the icy wall and I saw him. I felt his presence. Not in a literal sort of way, but in a powerful, uplifting, empowering way. From that moment, I felt his presence. At night, the clear sky was peppered with the most incredible starry spectacle. One star in particular always seemed to shine a little brighter, and it always brought me great comfort, particularly when we had a late-night climb.

When doubt enveloped me, I would simply look up at that star and I felt the power surge back through me. I don't know if it was a sense of purpose or a sense of companionship but thinking about him helped. Don't get me wrong, it wasn't overpowering. I thought about Ludo, Iona and Marina just as much, it's just that Willem helped overcome any sense of solitude. I never felt alone. I always felt like someone was watching over me.

Part of the helplessness of losing this little boy had been the lost dream. Here was a little boy who would never know the smell of popcorn, or the sweet taste of summer raspberries. He would never know Peppa Pig or the misery of car sickness. He would never know the taste of ice cream or the unpleasantness of Brussels sprouts. He would never know life. What would he have become, I used to wonder. What would he have done with his life?

As a father, my role is to nurture and protect and I always felt I failed Willem. Of course, nature works in her own way and Marina and I have always been pretty united behind the idea that what will be will be. I made a resolution when we lost Willem to ensure that we as a family lived our life to its full. I know it sounds like a cliché, but if you ever count up the days of frowns and cross words, they add up pretty quickly.

Marina and I decided we would live our lives more brightly. We would let them burn bright with light, happiness and opportunity, and it was from the embers of this huge fire that Everest had been born. I wanted to pursue my dreams. It's so easy to say no, there is always an excuse to not do something, but my new resolve was to seize the moment and live my life with no regrets.

It was just before 8 pm on the night that we attempted to climb to the top of the world. I hadn't slept. Rest had been fitful, the combination of the oxygen mask, fear and excitement had kept me awake for the couple of hours we had. I could already hear the crunch of crampons on the crisp new snow around the tents as early departures set off on their summit bids.

I pulled my mask from my face and slowly pulled myself from the warmth of the sleeping bag. My heart raced with even the minimum of exertion as I pulled on extra layers in the battle against the chill of the night. I unzipped the tent and stepped out into the night air. Camp 4 was a hive of activity as teams clipped on harnesses and crampons under the flickering light of their headlamps.

The night was windless and clear. It's amazing how much difference a day can make. Camp 4 had gone from wretched to benign. It felt safe and comfortable. I looked up towards the mountain flank of Everest and could already see a dozen lights on the mountainside. There were a further 20 climbers getting ready to leave.

I pulled on my harness and strapped my crampons to my summit boots. Although it was cold, it felt warmer without the wind chill of the previous day. I stepped from one foot to the next and leapt up and down until the thin air stole my breath. I slipped two bottles of 'O's' into my bag alongside a bottle of melted snow-water and a handful of snacks. Then I made sure I had my sunglasses and my goggles close by and pulled my summit mittens over my thin wool gloves. In the short time I had spent strapping my crampons onto my boots, I had already lost all feeling in my fingers. I wheeled my hand in a great circle to try and get the blood flowing into my numb digits.

I thought back to all the other expeditions over the years that had set off from this very point, full of hope, fear and aspirations of reaching the summit. So close and yet so far.

I thought about my family. They would be having their lunch now, oblivious to my departure for the highest point on earth.

Of course, I could have called them. I had my satellite phone. I was feeling good psychologically and physically, but it felt wrong. Why burden them with the fear of the unknown?

Up, from here the only way was Up.

I tried to imagine myself on the summit. I tried to drown out the 'down' that flooded through me like a raging river. I had to be positive, but once again the nagging voice of doubt took over.

'What if the weather turns unexpectedly again?' 'What if I can't climb a section because it's too technical?' 'What if someone dies while I am there?'

I was at risk of losing control of my mind. This was the battle of mind against mountain all over again.

Slowly, we trudged from the camp and down across a frozen glacial lake before beginning the long ascent up towards the famous Balcony. A single rope had been set up onto which the early departures had already begun their slow, meticulous climb.

It wasn't long before we reached the slow-moving group.

We had left at 8 pm, several hours earlier than Kenton normally departs for the eight-hour climb to the summit. We had hoped to get onto the mountain before the slower climbers snarled up the route. But we were already too late. Ahead of us was a queue of about 30 climbers, all from one very large Chinese group.

Our already slow pace was reduced to a standstill. It was a little like being stuck on the M25. We stood there for 15 minutes before taking several paces, followed by a further 15-minute wait. After an hour, we began to get restless. We wondered if there was an obstacle like a crevasse or even a steep climbing section somewhere up ahead that was acting like a bottleneck.

'Unclip from the rope and attach to me,' instructed Kenton.

I was sandwiched between two climbers. On the 60-degree slope, I unclipped from the mountain rope and using my crampons, dug my toes into the snow and pulled away from the long line of people.

We could now clearly see the long line snaking up the mountain, but there was no obvious sign of what was slowing everyone down.

I clipped onto Kenton's harness, and using his ice axe, Kenton began to crawl up the inside of the queue, dragging me behind him. From a near standstill, we were now suddenly making progress as we passed several climbers on the rope, but it didn't take long until the thin air left me gasping for breath. I collapsed onto all fours with the effort, panting deeply. In this short period of recovery, the slow-moving line inched ahead, effectively leaving us back where we had started.

We must have done this half a dozen times, each time overtaking one or two climbers.

It was as exhausting as it was soul-destroying. By now we had been trapped in the queue for nearly three hours.

'You need to turn your flow rate of oxygen down,' instructed Kenton. The flow rate dictated how much oxygen is released each minute. The higher the flow rate, the more oxygen you receive, the better you feel but the quicker it runs out. The lower the flow rate, the worse you feel but the longer it lasts.

I turned it down to one litre a minute and could already feel a drastic change in my breathing. We had several spare bottles, but they were to be 'cached' on the mountain ready for our descent.

I looked at my bottle which was already less than half full. We could still make out the lights from Camp 4, we had been on the mountain for three hours and we had barely made any headway.

How much oxygen did we have and how long would it last? I was worried. At this rate, we wouldn't get to the summit until early afternoon. It seemed hopeless.

'Is it worth turning back?' I asked Kenton in desperation.

He pointed out that if we did, we wouldn't be able to make

another summit bid as we didn't have enough oxygen at Camp 4. It was now or never.

Suddenly, I felt the summit slipping from my hands again. I felt a pang of anger and rage. Why were they moving so slowly? Why wouldn't they stop and let us pass? It felt so unfair. It wouldn't have taken them long to pull over. There was plenty of room and it was safe to do so. It would have taken five minutes.

I felt a surge of 'mountain rage'. 'DO YOU KNOW HOW MUCH EFFORT I HAVE PUT INTO THIS?' I wanted to shout. 'HAVE YOU ANY IDEA OF THE SACRIFICES I HAVE MADE? YOU HAVE NO IDEA WHAT THIS MEANS TO ME.'

I could feel my heart rate rising in anger and frustration.

Despite the agitation and harrumphing from the build-up of other climbers who were now queuing behind us, the group ahead continued at their snail's pace, unmoved, unbowed and unaffected by the frustrations behind.

Can you blame them? They too were pursuing their dreams and hopes, they too had made sacrifices.

By now we had been stuck for nearly four hours. It was after midnight and my first oxygen bottle was about to run out. On a normal ascent, it should have lasted nearly to the summit. We had to change the bottle on the line or risk being overtaken by the climbers behind us, pushing us even further back.

I knelt on my knees and Kenton dipped his gloves into my rucksack. With a swift movement, he pulled the empty bottle from my back, unscrewed the regulator and screwed it onto my spare bottle. This was the last of the bottles that I was carrying; another was in Sherpa Ang's bag.

Effortlessly, he screwed the new bottle onto the regulator and slipped it back into my bag. The whole thing had taken less than a minute. Time was running out though. It was nearly 1 am and we hadn't even reached the Balcony. Kenton suggested free climbing to pass the climbers ahead once again. My heart sank. I had found it difficult to recapture my breath each time we overtook some of the slow climbers.

I clenched my teeth and unclipped from the rope. Once again, Kenton clawed into the snow on all fours and began to work his way up past the slow climbers ahead. Four climbers, then two, then six. Before we knew it, there were just two climbers ahead of us.

'The Balcony is just ahead,' hollered Kenton as we overtook the final two Chinese climbers.

I collapsed onto all fours as we reached the tiny flat area, the only small respite on the summit ridge. I was gasping for air, even with my mask and oxygen, I was struggling to breathe. I fumbled for the supply valve and turned it up to the highest volume. It didn't help. I was like a goldfish, except each time I opened my mouth to breathe, it felt like nothing was going in.

I began to panic as I struggled for air. By now, the rest of the Chinese team were all arriving onto the Balcony. Panic turned to fear that they would pass us once again and we would lose all the ground that had taken us five hours to reclaim.

I sat on my rucksack and tried to inhale through my nose. Long, slow inhalations, followed by a long exhalation from my mouth. I thought back to the time I had spent in Thailand with Père Julian, the French-Canadian monk who had taught me breath control and meditation. I envisaged his little wooden meditation platform in the Thai jungle. I could see myself sitting there cross-legged, eyes closed, the sound of birdlife echoing through the jungle beyond as he taught me how to control my breathing.

'Smile and breathe in powerfully through your nose for 20 seconds,' he had instructed me. 'Now hold the breath and then exhale for 30 seconds.'

It's amazing the power of the mind. In that moment, I left the Balcony and returned to Thailand. I could feel my heart slowing, and gradually I regained control of my breathing. It was scary how quickly and how easily I had lost control in the first place.

'The Balcony. I'm on the famous Balcony,' I thought to myself, as finally my senses returned.

By now, dozens of climbers had arrived on this narrow patch of snow. Not prepared to be overtaken by the same climbers we had spent more than five hours trying to overtake, we started almost immediately on the next stage of our ascent.

I took the lead at the head of the group as I clipped onto the line and headed into the darkness. The route led me along a sharp pinnacle of snow with steep drops on either side. In the gloom, it was difficult to tell how far they fell.

Carefully, I placed one foot in front of the other as I navigated the thin ledge. I could already see the headlights of the team behind us, assembling on the line. It felt like we had control of the situation again. The summit was in our grasp. I had plenty of oxygen on a low delivery. I was feeling confident and we had a clear mountain ahead of us; what's more, the sky was still clear, with the promise of good weather ahead.

My mind began to drift to the summit and the feeling of relief.

It was too soon.

Psssttttt ...

There was a loud, high-pitched hissing coming from behind me. The sudden break from the silence made me jump from my daydreams. My heart started to race as I turned to see where the noise was coming from. It was deafeningly loud, but I couldn't make out its source. Each time I turned, the noise seemed to stay with me.

In my oxygen-starved brain, it was difficult to work out what was happening. Suddenly, a moment of realisation. It was coming from me. It was coming from my bag. It was my oxygen. I stopped as the others caught up. I slipped the rucksack off my shoulders and placed it on the ground. Had Kenton forgotten to screw the regulator onto the bottle properly? Had I knocked the top of the bottle, loosening the valve?

I couldn't compute what had gone wrong. Why was my bottle spewing my precious, life-saving, beautiful oxygen into the thin air? We were well into the death zone at about 8,500 metres and my lifeline was disappearing before me. I pulled the mask from my face as the last wisps of oxygen disappeared into the chill mountain air.

'Breathe deep,' I repeated to myself, 'breathe slowly.'

I could feel panic rising from inside, but once again I tried to withdraw internally back to that little platform in Thailand.

'It's the regulator that's blown,' explained Kenton as he unscrewed the tether from the bottle. Somehow the D-ring that connects the regulator to the bottle had blown, allowing the contents of my bottle to leak out.

It was the worst news possible. If it had been one of the bottles themselves that had leaked, then I could simply have used another one. But it wasn't. It was the regulator that connects the mask to the bottle and it had blown irreparably. We didn't carry spares. I couldn't see how I was going to get out of this one. Without a spare regulator, it would be difficult to go anywhere.'

There is a misconception that climbing Everest without oxygen is a common thing to do. It is not. Climbing Everest without 'O's' is a feat completed by the few. Indeed, of the 4,000 people to have climbed to the summit, fewer than 200 have done so without oxygen. That's only five per cent.

Of course, those 200 climbers who have successfully ascended without oxygen have done so with either years of practice or an extraordinary metabolism. After days of dependency on oxygen, to suddenly take it away would be a little like free-diving without oxygen tanks to twice the usual depth.

Going slowly, I estimated I could probably descend back to Camp 4 where we would be able to radio for help from below to bring a spare up from Base Camp, but even this seemed risky.

Supplementary oxygen ensures the blood remains warm and that it circulates in the body keeping all extremities like fingers, toes and nose warm in the extreme cold. Many of the cases of frostbite that have afflicted so many climbers over the years are the result of being caught in storms and their oxygen running out. The combination of long exposure to the cold and the lack of oxygen, invariably leads to frostbite injury.

The second symptom of lack of oxygen is a confused state of mind and disorientation. Even with supplementary oxygen, I was struggling to stay focused and in control. I didn't have too long to worry. Kenton turned to Ming Dorjee Sherpa. 'Will you give your bottle and regulator to Ben and go back to Camp 4?'

It was a big ask and naturally Ming Dorjee wasn't sure. For many of the sherpas, the summit day is payday. They can earn more in a single summit from the 'summit bonus' than most Nepalese earn in a year. Many sherpas will spend years working up to the summit. It is the sum of their ambition. What's more, it's an investment in their future employment prospects. Sherpas who have summited before are usually more coveted. The more summits the more work; it's a profession after all.

To ask Ming Dorjee to give up his summit for me was a massive thing to request of him. Effectively, he would be sacrificing his own success for mine.

'I'll still pay you the summit bonus,' I implored.

He looked at me and then at Kenton. 'Okay,' he nodded.

It was a selfless act of heroism. I felt quite emotional as he handed me his mask and bottle.

Ming Dorjee began the slow, painful journey without oxygen or a mask back to Camp 4. Meanwhile, we were once again heading up the mountain.

It was still pitch black as we continued our ascent. By now, the Chinese team were once again hot on our heels, closing in on us as we marched onwards.

The very first, faint outline of light had appeared on the horizon. It painted the line between the mountains and the sky with a dull orange hue. At first it was almost imperceptible, but as the morning marched forwards it turned to violet and then purple.

Soon I could see a perfect outline of the peaks in the distance, their contours silhouetted vividly against the dawn colours. It was just after 4 am and there was enough light to climb without a headtorch. We reached a vertiginous section of ice and rock that soared high above. For the first time since leaving Camp 4, I could see the scale of our exposure on the mountain.

I looked up and the little voice of self-doubt returned as I clipped onto another rope that soared high into the thin air.

'Look Up,' I kept repeating to myself, 'don't look down.'

It took all I could to control my fear as my crampons dug into the hard ice. Occasionally, I didn't 'toe' the crampons hard enough and one boot would slip. It was terrifying.

One boot in front of the other. Slowly, I made a little headway up the icy slope until we reached a small wall of rock. Just as I was about to haul myself over it, I heard another loud bang.

Psssstttttt …

My heart sank as I turned to see where it was coming from. I felt sure it must be me again. How could this be happening? The noise sounded a little more distant than last time. I grabbed my regulator and looked at the gauge. It appeared normal. Where was the noise coming from? Looking behind me, I saw that Mark was struggling. He had taken his pack off. It was Mark's bottle. The D-ring had blown and his precious oxygen was gone.

What the hell was happening? Kenton had reassured us that in 12 summits he had never experienced equipment failure with the oxygen bottles or the regulators, and now here we were at 8,700 metres dealing with our second explosion. My heart raced as panic began to bubble. What if my bottle also goes? And Kenton's and Ang Thindu's?

Once again, I was losing the battle of mind over mountain. We were on one of the most exposed slopes on the climb, a sheer icy cliff with drops of thousands of metres below us. For the first time since crossing one of the ice ladders in the Khumbu Icefall, I felt a surge of vertigo envelop my body. I froze. I daren't look down.

This time it was Ang Thindu who came to the rescue. Fearful that I would be overwhelmed by vertigo, I decided that the only way was up. If I stayed while the team swapped bottles and equipment, I was fearful that I would be overcome by my fear of heights.

'Carry on and we'll catch you up,' hollered Kenton.

Slowly and meticulously, I carried on alone. Higher and higher I climbed until soon the team were out of sight.

I found myself perched alone on an exposed shoulder of the mountain. The sun had just broken over the horizon, casting a giant shadow of Everest onto the peaks beyond. It was without doubt the finest, the most glorious, the most otherworldly sunrise I have ever witnessed.

I was alone. Marooned high on the mountain.

Before long Kenton and Mark rejoined me and we continued towards the summit.

I could make out a large flat surface above me, shimmering in the early morning glow of light. The summit. It must be the summit.

How I had longed for this moment.

Head down, I climbed as hard as I could to reach that seemingly impossible place. That tiny point of snow and ice that has claimed so many lives.

Just a few more paces and I was on the roof …

Hang on. As I looked ahead of me, I could see that the snowy slope continued along a jagged ridge.

It was a false peak. Otherwise known as the south summit.

The north summit, the real peak, was on the other side of the jagged, crown-like ridge.

'How long do you think it will take us?' I asked Kenton against my better judgement. I had always avoided the 'How long until …' question. The answer was always bad. Ever since I was a child, I have hated the answer. I prefer the unknown.

'About an hour and a half.'

I would have preferred the unknown.

About an hour and a half. But I was done. I had no gas left in the tank. I had peaked too early. It looked impossible and the inner voice of doubt returned.

We rested next to a wall of rock. This was where Rob Hall made his last phone call before perishing in the 1996 tragedy.

After some Haribo and some Maltesers, we soldiered on along the crest of the ridge.

'Whoa Ben, not so close to the edge,' warned Kenton. 'It's an overhang.'

It soon became apparent just how vulnerable we were as we climbed up and down the jagged icy ridge that led towards the summit. The north summit. The true summit that I could now see clearly in the distance.

But first we had to cross the infamous Hillary Step.

Much has been made about the Hillary Step since the earthquake of 2015. There had been plenty of reports that part of the rock had crumbled away leaving more of a ramp than a step. But without a proper geological survey, there is still some debate about how much it has changed.

Having nothing to compare it with, I had to rely on Kenton to explain that the upper part had indeed crumbled away, leaving a series of steep steps. What had once been a dangerous bottleneck was now just dangerous.

The summit suddenly looked like it was in my grasp again.

I took a large step up.

Pssssttttt ...

That dreadful sound will remain with me until the day I die, which quite frankly felt like it was now.

That hideous, high-pitched squeal and squeak as my lifeline of oxygen fizzed and evaporated from the bottle – my second regulator had blown. My oxygen had disappeared into the thin air. I was at 8,800 metres and I was out of my depth. Nothing had prepared me for this. Nothing. I had nothing to draw on. Helpless. Hopeless. Senseless.

I began to panic. I lost my breath. I was having a panic attack. In the thin air, I couldn't think straight. Kenton and Mark were there. Reassuring. Kenton was quick. He ripped his own mask from his face and placed it over my mouth.

What about Kenton? What would he do now? Could he descend from here without oxygen? Was he capable? Could we go on without him? So many questions, but all of them drowned out by the intoxication of being just 50 metres from the summit.

'You go on,' insisted Kenton. 'I'll catch you up.'

He explained that his best hopes of a spare bottle would be on the summit where there would be more climbers from both sides of the mountain. I looked at Kenton, turned towards the summit and started climbing. Further up, I looked back at Kenton to see him on his hands and knees.

'What have I done?'

Marina – Breaking radio silence

Finally, there was some news. A text.

'It looks like we'll be leaving on Thursday morning, early. I'll call you on Wednesday.'

My anxiety was beginning to build. I feared not only that he wouldn't be safe, but also that he might have to face failure and return to the UK, defeated.

Wednesday came and went with no call from Ben. I consoled myself that no news was good news. As used as we are to being in constant communication, you were at nature's mercy at the foot of Everest. Sometimes the internet worked and you had phone signal, sometimes it didn't, and there wasn't anything anyone could do about it.

On Friday morning, the familiar sat-phone number flashed up on my screen. It was Ben calling from Camp 2. He told me that there had been a huge electrical storm and the communications at Base Camp had been completely offline. He maintained that he was feeling good, strong and excited about their summit attempt, but I could hear the exhaustion in his voice. As we talked he rasped, and between our breathless exchanges, his hacking cough reminded me that life at that altitude is not sustainable to human existence.

They had identified a weather window on Monday morning. 'I can't promise I'll call you from the top,' he warned. I got that, but still, I was going to make damn sure that my phone was right beside me through the night.

CNN, who were filming the expedition, wanted me to record any phone call I might have with my husband from the top. Neil, who was leading the production, came to set up a small GoPro and show me how to use it. I was distracted, this seemed presumptuous and I didn't want to spend too long thinking how to record a phone call which I wasn't sure I was ever going to receive. They asked me to take the cameras wherever I went, something I ignored resolutely.

CHAPTER TWELVE

SUMMIT

I could barely lift one foot in front of the other. I was reduced to dragging my following foot to save energy. Neil Armstrong walking on the moon looked like Usain Bolt compared to my speed. I would walk a couple of paces and then have to stop to get my breath back. I have never in my life felt so depleted of energy or restricted of ability. It was like I had been wrapped in chains.

I could see the north summit up ahead. I could make out the brightly coloured suits of half a dozen climbers. Where had they come from? I knew we were the first climbers to reach the summit. We had passed everyone else and I was pretty sure there had been no one ahead of us. In my exhaustion, I had failed to remember that half the summiteers had come up from the north side. These climbers ahead of me had come from the China side.

The summit was within touching distance and yet it never seemed to get closer as I edged along the narrow crest of

mountain towards the highest point on earth. Mark was now a
short distance ahead of me. I looked around and there was no
sign of Kenton, nor any other climbers.

I shuffled and gasped and wheezed and suffered up to that last
tiny stretch of hill until finally I reached the prayer flags that
marked the top of the world at 8,848 metres.

This was it. From this little mound, it was impossible to go any
higher unless you were in a flying machine.

I was on the roof of the world.

Strangely, there was no fist-pumping euphoria. There were no
hollers of success or tears of emotion. In fact, I felt slightly
emotionless. It was hyper-real. Even now. It remains one of the
most vivid experiences of my life. It was like every sense had been
turned to maximum level, and yet, despite the intenseness of the
moment, I felt numb. There was nothing. No relief. No happiness.
No elation. Nothing.

I sat there, on that little mound of snow and ice, and I stared
out at the landscape beyond. The sky was so blue it looked black.
I felt closer to space than I did to anywhere recognisable. Up here,
I could make out the curvature of the earth. Next time you are in
a commercial airliner cruising at altitude, imagine climbing out
of the window and sitting on the wing. This was my view. The
mountains below stretched, unbroken, for hundreds of miles. I
couldn't see a sign of mankind. For 360 degrees, snowy peaks and
glaciers disappeared into the curved horizon.

To describe it as breathtaking doesn't really do it justice. It was
so unlike any vista I had ever experienced before that I had no
terms of reference. Many of these mountains far below me, were
6,000- and 7,000-metre peaks – anywhere else on the planet they

would be dominating the geography, but here at nearly 9,000 metres, they were dwarfed by Everest. The surrounding Himalayas looked Lilliputian. I felt an insignificant, inconsequential dot in this vast, overwhelming landscape.

The vividness of that experience will haunt me forever. It was like taking drugs. My senses were heightened and I had moments of intense lucidity. The contradiction between hyper reality and numbness was even more surreal. I placed my rucksack on the ground and removed my oxygen mask from my face to give me more freedom to take in the magnitude of the place.

The sky was crystal clear. There was very little wind and the sun was beating down on us. It felt so safe and benign. It was calm and surreal. This was not the image I had in my mind of the exposed summit.

I looked around in a daze. Confused and overwhelmed. No experience had ever had this impact. For the first time in my life, I wasn't armed to cope with the situation. I felt powerless and rudderless and yet … And yet it was like my epiphany. It was like a direct shaft of light from high above was shining onto me. Empowering me.

By now, more and more climbers from the south had started to arrive at the summit, and in the distance I could make out Kenton making even slower progress than I had.

The summit itself is a pretty small area with precipitous drops all around. Unclipped as I was, I was pretty vulnerable as we all jostled for space. The calm, good weather and the gathering crowd created a carnival-like feeling. For some strange reason, I had the image of the fairground scene from *Mary Poppins*, the one in which they leap through the chalk drawing.

Finally, Kenton emerged from the slope. Three paces and he was there, with us on the summit. Kenton, Mark and I all hugged. It was a profoundly moving experience. I had shared this most intense experience with these two men. They had been my guides and my companions, my friends and my protectors. In those final metres, Kenton had risked his own life to save mine in the ultimate act of selfless heroism.

For Kenton, it was his 13th summit. Unlucky for some. I knew this one had been bugging him. He missed out on a summit the previous year, and like me, there had been so many moments on this climb when he thought we were doomed.

For Mark, it was his first Everest summit. He had done it so effortlessly, always with a smile on his face. Never complaining, never fearful, never compromising. He had been one of the best mountain companions I could ever have asked for. Not only had he climbed Everest with ease, but he had done so with camera in hand.

I loved these guys. We had done this together. I thought of Victoria. Where was she now? I wished she was here with us, on the summit of the tallest mountain on earth. So many lives, almost 300, have been lost in the pursuit of this tiny little place. So many families torn apart and lives shattered. All of that just to stand, fleetingly, in this haunting, otherworldly spot. Why had I made it? Why had I been allowed to stand here, on this little patch of snow that had defied so many before me?

Some say Everest is easy. It's certainly a whole lot easier and safer now than it was for those early pioneering climbers who were confronted with a virgin mountain. It is only because of their heroics that people like me stand a chance of summiting. But it is not easy. Not by any stretch of the imagination.

It may not be technical. We may rely on the vital help of the sherpas. There may be a rope to follow all the way to the top. Easier, maybe. Not easy.

I think that part of my reticence to celebrate was that we were only really halfway. What goes up must come down and we still had the long, dangerous descent to Base Camp. Kenton had recommended preserving 25 to 30 per cent of my energy to get back. To be honest, I probably had a little less than that. The exhaustion of the climb combined with the terror of the exploding oxygen bottles had drained me physically and mentally.

Many climbers before me have failed to allow for the descent. So focused and obsessed with the summit, they become blinded to what has to follow. Normally sensible becomes crazily irrational, and up here in the death zone, the results are invariably death. More people have died on the descent of Everest than during the climb to the top.

I had promised Marina that I would put common sense and self-preservation before any ego-obsessed desire to summit. One of my favourite quotes is from Sir Ernest Shackleton who turned back just a hundred miles from the South Pole. Unlike his contemporary Captain Scott, Shackleton knew that if he carried on in vainglory to the Pole, he would run out of supplies for the return journey.

Upon returning to Britain, his wife asked him why he turned back when so close to the South Pole. 'Better a live donkey than a dead lion,' he replied.

There are many dead lions on Everest and I wasn't prepared to be one of them.

I wanted to call Marina from the summit. I had a satellite phone with me and I was desperate to share this moment with her. Although she was thousands of miles away with my family, she was as much a part of this journey as I was. I might have put in the physical effort, but Marina had the mental fortitude, willing me on and keeping the family together.

I wasn't sure if it was bad karma to call her. After all, I still had many days of climbing ahead of me. But I decided I needed to hear her voice.

'I'm here,' I whispered hoarsely down the phone. 'I'm on the summit.'

Even in my slightly brain-frazzled state, it seemed incredible that I was talking to my wife. It was 3 am in the UK and she would be tucked up in bed. It felt utterly surreal to be speaking to her from atop Everest.

'It was really hard,' I added before breaking into uncontrollable sobs. The emotion was overwhelming. I wished my whole family could see this moment. To feel it. To experience it.

It felt life changing and life affirming at the same time, but then a huge part of it was the circumstances. Every person who summits Everest will experience powerfully unique sentiments, often products of their own unique lives.

Marina – The summit

They say no news is good news, but when your husband is scaling Everest, I'm just not sure this is the case. Ben's Instagram feed had been full of photos of his preparation. He'd used the extraordinary scenery and his time for reflection to post pictures that gripped his followers' attention. I'd got used to seeing three or four posts every day, the long words that accompanied them betraying the time he had to gather his thoughts. Because of the electrical storm that had hit Base Camp on his last day, he hadn't told his followers that he was off, and so his family and his followers, on the edge of their seats, were plunged into an unanticipated silence.

I held my breath over the weekend, filling every idle moment with podcasts so my mind had less opportunity to wander. While out running, I pushed myself harder than I ever had before. However exhausted my well-nourished body seemed, it was nothing compared to what my husband was enduring.

Sunday night came and I knew that if they summited on Monday morning, I would probably get a call around 3 am my time. I set up the GoPro that CNN had given me, checked my phone was not on silent and tried to go to sleep. I tossed and turned, fluctuating between sleeplessness and nightmares. In an attempt to stop my mind from whirring, I put on an audiobook. The only one I had was Fire and Fury, *the account of Trump's election victory and first few months in the White House. Incorporating an orange-hued comedy character in charge of the Western world, my nightmares took on an even darker theme. That was not going to work.*

I awoke at 6 am, the realisation that there had been no phone call hitting me like a bullet in the stomach. Did that mean he didn't get there, did it mean they'd had an accident? I dropped the children at school, my smile rigid and insincere as I breezed that, no, I hadn't heard anything yet.

That afternoon, Tamara, Ben's sister, dropped by to see how I was doing. My smile was still pasted rigidly to my face. My phone pinged, it was from a sat-phone. 'Safely at C4. A bit windy. Gonna rest an extra day here before summit bid. Love you xxxx.' I read it about 10 times. That initial rush of relief was soon replaced by the nagging feeling that something was wrong. I knew enough about Everest to understand that you didn't have a rest day at Camp 4. At 8,000 metres, it was in the death zone, where the body starts to deteriorate rapidly, the brain and body shutting down due to the lack of oxygen. One of the things that had reassured me most was that weather prediction was now a lot more reliable, meaning that storms that hit out of the blue, like the one in 1996 which claimed eight lives on one night, should no longer happen. If bad weather had hit, why on earth were they even up there?

I couldn't get the message out of my head. I'd responded immediately, but there had been no further contact. 'Gonna rest an extra day' did not sound like Ben. In the nearly 15 years we'd known each other, I'd never heard him say, let alone write, 'gonna'. Was it even him texting?

My biggest fear was obviously that he'd be injured or die on that mountain. But I had another real and persistent worry, that he'd fail. It takes great courage to embark on an expedition of this magnitude, one in which luck plays a huge role. But it takes even more guts to attempt something like this when many millions are following you.

Ben has always been wise when it comes to failure. 'Mistakes are only negative when you don't learn from them' is a mantra often repeated in our household. We embrace them, thankful that nature has a great way of making damn sure you don't make the same mistake twice.

On holiday in Sri Lanka, we'd talked a lot about the concept of failure. Our children love the stories of the old explorers and so Ben told them all about Shackleton and Scott. They learned about the race to the South Pole, to be the first to stand on the ice-hewn most southern point of our planet. About Shackleton, who early on realised that his dream was not going to come true and instead focused on getting his team back safely. And Scott, who in blind determination persevered and did finally get to the Pole, but having sacrificed his and much of his team's lives. We asked them who they felt the real hero was among these polar pioneers.

Ludo and Iona were resolutely on Shackleton's side. We used this to illustrate that turning around, making what is often a difficult decision, is often braver and more courageous than to continue blindly. I said that we'd celebrate Ben's return as gleefully regardless of whether he got to the summit or not. And while I was good at articulating

*what in principle I believed to be true, I feared what
returning without having summited would do to Ben.*

*The pressure intensified when Ben realised a few weeks
before he left that his film crew would not be the only one on
the mountain. Ant Middleton would be there too, making a
documentary for Channel 4. At first, I dismissed this as idle
gossip. There was nothing on his frequently updated social
media channels. Why, if he was planning such an exciting
expedition, did he not share this with his army of followers?*

*It turned out that they were not only sharing an ambition,
but a camp as well. I could sense Ben's frustration that
within a handful of tents perched at the end of Base Camp,
two film crews were jostling for attention. Having a
competitor at your heels might well inspire resolve, bravery
and persistence, but it might also spur Ben on to make
foolish decisions. I cursed bloody Ant Middleton for being
there.*

*That summit week, with virtually no cohesive
communication, no way of knowing where the team were,
what their plans were and what the weather was doing, were
some of the hardest days of my life. Why hadn't Ben worn a
tracker so I could at least find out where he was on the
mountain? I had no contact at Base Camp, no way of
knowing what on earth was happening to my husband. By
Tuesday, they'd been up on the mountain for six days. I knew
that most summit bids took around five days but could often
be done a lot quicker. Kenton had summited and got down
to Base Camp in one day. Ben had been at Camp 2 on
Friday. Why the hell hadn't he summited yet?*

As resolute that my decision not to google was, I still listened to the radio where I learned that Xia Boyu, a 69-year-old Chinese double amputee, had summited on Monday. What the hell was Ben doing faffing around at Camp 4 while a pensioner with no legs managed to climb it, I thought ungraciously.

On Tuesday, Ben's agent called me to say that she'd had an unconfirmed report that Ant had made it. And still no word from Ben. My fear that he hadn't made it was consuming me by now. And with it I anticipated the disappointment that would inevitably consume Ben on his return. The more I thought about it, the more I battled with how unfair that would be.

I thought about sending Ben an e-mail. I wanted him to know that we would be equally proud of him whether or not he summited. Any disappointment he felt would not be felt by us. I wanted to confirm that I wanted to add a caveat into my agreement to let him climb Everest. That he return home positive, triumphant and grateful for the opportunity, no matter what the outcome. 'I can endure the weeks you spend away from us, the time we're apart, the school plays, assemblies and parents evenings I only ever go to on my own. I can deal with lonely weekends, with Sunday nights spent persuading over-tired children to go to sleep before packing uniform, PE kit and swimming gear for the week ahead with no help, the evenings with no one to chat about my day with, or concerns about the kids. I can deal with the ever-growing collection of coats, crampons and summit suits that are invading our house. I can deal with the sleepless nights, the feigned cheerfulness when all I want to do is sob hot tears of worry. I can even deal with the Daily Mail *calling me up with passive-aggressive suggestions that my husband is furtively having a steamy affair with his climbing partner as they share a tent together. But what I can't deal with, is if the man whose return we've been anticipating, dreaming of, for the last two months, is tinged with self-induced disappointment. If the joy felt by us as we hug the person we've missed with every inch of our beating hearts, is not reciprocated; if the celebration of your return is in any way soured by the fact that you didn't reach the summit, you will have let us all down. So, when we see you, whatever the outcome, we need a smile and for you to wholeheartedly discard any disappointment that you might feel.'*

I never pressed send, but writing it, released a great deal of anxiety I'd been harbouring. If it didn't go to plan, at least I had a plan and could warn him that he'd better bloody have a smile on his face.

By the end of the Tuesday, dizzy with tiredness I collapsed into bed, falling asleep with my book on my chest, Storm, my faithful bed companion, lying at my feet. I awoke abruptly to the sound of my phone ringing. Ben's sat-phone. I scrambled to answer it. 'Hello?' I asked cautiously. The line crackled and then, choked with emotion, I heard Ben's voice. 'We did it, my darling, we did it.' Between sobs Ben told me how this was the hardest thing he'd ever done. He tried to describe the beauty of the world set out in front of him, his voice breaking with the emotion of having achieved something he doubted he'd be able to do.

We spoke for a few minutes. While I didn't want to rush him, I also knew how important it was not to spend too much time at the summit, before the descent, arguably more perilous than the ascent. He said that they were planning to get back to Camp 2 that day and he'd try and call me when he got there.

I put my phone down, relief flooded through me and hot tears of gratitude cascaded down my cheeks.

The one thing I felt guilty about was that I hadn't managed to record the phone call. I'm not great with technology at the best of times, but awoken suddenly at 3 am with a phone call that represented one of the biggest tipping points in my life, I'd failed to work the goddamn camera. I hadn't though told the children, who slept peacefully upstairs. The stress had impacted them and I didn't feel I could interrupt their much-needed sleep. The news could wait until the morning.

We're early risers in our house – school starts at 8 am and since breakfast usually takes an hour, we have no choice. Getting the children out of bed though is getting harder and harder. It's often impossible to get them to leave their cosy cocoons to get dressed and get to school. On this day though, it would be different.

As I opened their shutters, I whispered that I had some exciting news for them. 'Come downstairs to my bedroom and I'll tell you,' I urged. They needed no encouragement, racing down and leaping onto my bed, their faces flushed with anticipation.

'So, I had a call from Daddy at 3 o'clock in the morning,' I

told them, 'and guess where he was?' 'The top of Everest?'
they asked. I nodded as they yelped with joy. This time I'd
managed to press record and when Ben returned to Base
Camp and the internet, he saw the video of the moment his
children learned of their Daddy's achievement.

For an hour we stood, stared, took pictures, hugged and cried.
Just before we began our long journey back down the mountain,
I dipped into my rucksack and fished out the squeaky carrot and
the panda bear known as Pandear which Ludo and Iona had
chosen to accompany me up the mountain. I held them aloft as
Mark took a photo for my children.

Despite the solitude, I had never really been alone. Willem, my
little boy lost, had always been there. I looked up at the sky and
whispered a thank you, the words disappearing into the ether.

By now, the summit was getting really crowded. Soon they
would all be beginning their own slow descents. We didn't want
to get stuck behind another long line of people. The sun was
already heating up and we only had a limited supply of oxygen.

Kenton had managed to borrow a spare bottle and mask from
a fellow climber.

For the first time in a week, we were finally descending. There
was a slight euphoria in the knowledge that at least we would be
going with gravity, but now we had the added difficulty of a busier
route and soft snow and ice.

A long line of climbers were working their way along the narrow fin of ice from the south summit up to the north summit. This is often a bottleneck and requires ruthless confidence, if you want to avoid being stuck for hours.

In the harsh glow of full daylight, under the glaring sun, the exposure of the summit suddenly became dizzying. Kenton had warned me to keep away from the edge on the ascent, but it was only now that I could see this small fin of wind-blown ice was all that separated me from the 3,000-metre drop to Tibet below.

Vertiginous drops on either side suddenly transformed what had been a slog coming up, into a terrifying obstacle course.

As I approached each climber coming up the narrow ledge, there would invariably be a hesitation. Surprisingly, there are no hard and fast rules on the mountain. No right of way or even mountain etiquette. I decided to use confidence.

Leaving the ascending mountaineer fully clipped to the mountain rope, I would grab their hand or harness with my hand while sliding past them and re-clipping on the other side.

It sometimes necessitated a somewhat exposed and vulnerable manoeuvre, which meant more haste but also more safety, as I was in control of the situation.

I became pretty efficient at passing both those ascending and descending. If there was one thing I had learned on the mountain in the previous few months, it was to never languish behind the slower climbers.

The heat by now was starting to build and I found myself removing layer upon layer until I was in just a thin wool thermal. It seemed incredible that I was way above 8,700 metres in the death zone, where plenty of people have perished from exposure over the years, and yet I was wearing little more than a T-shirt.

While I had been looking forward to the comparative 'ease' of the descent, what you gain in gravity, you lose in stability. The slowness of the ascent was more conducive to careful control. The haste and fatigue of the descent has often led to tragedy on the mountain.

One misplaced foot or mis-clipped carabiner could be fatal.

My legs were like jelly. I had already lost a tremendous amount of muscle mass in the weeks on the mountain, and now the weight of my backpack together with the exhaustion of nearly two days in the death zone were beginning to take their toll.

We would break our descent into two stages. First, we would make our way down to Camp 4 where we would take a rehydrated meal and melt some snow before descending past Camp 3 to Camp 2. The whole thing could take us up to 12 hours. One hell of a day.

At the bottom of the south summit, Mark and I took a break near a wall of rock. The route was bustling with new arrivals. By now, the fin of ice appeared to be one long line of climbers. It was a slightly surreal sight. I was glad to be out of the melee.

We could see Kenton descending against the flow of those heading towards the summit. We waited for him to reach us and then together we began the long climb down.

We didn't stop until we reached the Balcony. I sat down as the sun beat down on me and looked out at the astonishing view beyond. A handful of other climbers were also resting. We all sat there in silence. Defeated by exhaustion.

From here we retraced our steps down the sheer slope on which we had spent five hours on the ascent stuck behind the group of Chinese climbers. What a difference a few hours made. It was unrecognisable in the sunshine of the day. It was also a great deal steeper than I remembered.

For two hours we descended the perilous slope. My knees burnt with the effort. My toes bruised as they were hammered into the front of my boots. I could feel toenails being ripped from my toes by the pressure and weight of my steps.

Without warning, my foot slipped. I lost control and balance and my body lurched downwards. I flailed out with my ice axe, but my foot kept slipping. Why wasn't my crampon holding? I looked down to see a bare boot and no sign of a crampon.

Something as simple as a lost crampon can be the difference between life and death. Above 8,000 metres, everything matters, every little detail counts and losing a crampon could have a defining impact on the rest of the journey.

In fact, the loss of a crampon would make a descent almost impossible. I still had one crampon and I had seen sherpas climbing with just one, but in the icy conditions of the descent, I needed all the grip and leverage I could get.

I panicked as my eyes scanned the slope for my missing crampon. A couple of metres away, reflecting in the harsh sunlight, was the missing piece of kit. My heart leapt. Salvation.

It never ceased to amaze me the peaks and troughs between drama and euphoria each day. The altitude seemed to have a powerful effect on the brain and the combination led to high anxiety, tension and emotion.

I let myself slide down the hill until I reached the missing crampon. Carefully I reached out with my gloved hand and scooped it up. Having been reunited, I now had to somehow fit it back onto my boot.

The gradient was nearly 70 per cent. I couldn't sit without slipping, let alone gain enough purchase with the sole of my crampon-less boot. I dug away at the snow with my boot to make a little ledge on which I would be able to put pressure on the crampon on the steep slope.

The problem was that each time I pushed, the soft snow and ice gave way until I slipped further down the mountain. Fortunately, I was still clipped to the rope which prevented me plunging hundreds of metres down the flanks of Everest.

I could feel panic and anxiety bubbling up from within. It felt like I was losing control of the situation. It is amazing how the smallest of errors can steal your confidence.

From the elation of standing on the summit, I had been reduced to a panicking wreck on the side of the mountain and all because I was struggling to re-attach my crampon.

Eventually, Kenton and Mark arrived to help. Kenton told me to use my jumar to take my weight off the rope, to give me more mobility in my leg. It was so obvious and so simple, but in my confused exhaustion it had become an unsolvable puzzle.

That descent seemed to go on forever. How I longed for it to end. My mouth was parched. I hadn't drunk anything since my water bottle had frozen solid, which had been about an hour after leaving Camp 4 the previous night.

We could see Camp 4, long before we reached her tattered tents. For almost the entire climb up the mountain, I had been dreaming about the time we would be going down, but now, in the midst of it, I couldn't wait for it to end. The pain from my toes and knees was unforgiving.

A couple of hours after leaving the summit, I slumped into our three-man tent. I lay there. Comatose. Unable to move. I stared at the top of the tent. I was done. Spent. I had used up all the spares I had.

I was too tired to eat or drink. My back was aching from my heavy pack, which had picked up weight after Ang Thindu and Ming Dorjee had given us their oxygen and returned to Camp 4.

I didn't want to move. The problem was that we had already spent longer than we had wanted above 8,000 metres. The death zone, as its name suggests, is not somewhere to hang out. We had already been in the death zone for more than two days and if we stayed it would be a further day.

Despite our lethargy and exhaustion, Kenton suggested we carry on to the comparative safety of Camp 2 where we would have food and more oxygen.

Weird things can happen on a mountain. As a child, I was obsessed with the Yeti, or Abominable Snowman as he is known locally. It was during the descent that something very strange happened. I had been on my feet for nearly 20 hours. I had sustained myself on a sip of water and a couple of Jelly Babies and was close to collapsing with exhaustion.

I was halfway between Camp 4 and Camp 3 and the weather had turned. A strong wind had enveloped the mountain and visibility had been reduced to just a few metres.

Tired and consumed with fatigue, I had become slovenly with

my safety. Occasionally, I would check down at my safety harness only to realise that I had forgotten to clip it to the line.

To speed up my descent, I would often wrap the rope around my arm and use it as a brake as I lowered myself down the steep icy slope. We had spread out a little – Mark and Kenton were a little behind me, higher up the mountain and out of sight – and I was alone for the moment.

As I descended, I noticed something ahead of me. I saw the silhouette of someone walking towards me, a little more than 20 metres down the slope. Something was wrong though. Their head was oversized. Ridiculously oversized, like a giant balloon. It must be someone carrying something on their head, I thought to myself, as I continued to stare at this strange vision. As it came closer to me, I could make out a shaggy mop of hair on its massive head and its massive hands also covered in fur.

I was dumbfounded. Even in my state of exhaustion, I could make out the figure quite clearly. It looked like one of the monsters from *Where the Wild Things Are*. It was so clear. I stared at it. Not with fear but confusion. As the beast got closer to me, I could make out its teeth and huge, oversized eyes.

I stood there rooted to the spot. I pulled my sunglasses off and rubbed my eyes. I looked again and there in front of me, just a few metres away, was a slightly startled climber. He was perfectly normal in size, with a large pack on his back.

We nodded at one another as I passed him on the rope.

It had been a hallucination. My first and last on Everest. It had been so powerfully realistic that I couldn't help but wonder if some of the Yeti sightings over the years had been imagined by equally exhausted mountaineers. Was this a final parting shot from the mountain in the battle of minds and bodies?

Marina – Life after Everest

One thing I was unprepared for was how quickly Ben would descend from the summit and be back home. In the early hours on Wednesday he was speaking to me from the roof of the world and three days later he was back in our arms, feet firmly at sea-level in London.

While the world sat in front of their televisions to watch Prince Harry and Meghan Markle tie the knot, I drove our little family to Heathrow, our car stuffed with signs that the children had lovingly made in anticipation of their father's return. The spring sun shone fiercely, showing our green and pleasant land off in all her glory, verdant green clashing with Union Jack bunting fluttering in the gentle breeze. It was one of those days that makes you joyful to be alive and I couldn't wait to finally hold the man I'd missed and worried about and so needed over the past few months.

Buzzing with excitement, the children skipped into the airport, clutching their 'Welcome Home Daddy' placards. We gathered with a good view of the arrivals door and kept a fierce eye on the weary travellers pushing their trolleys towards us. And then I finally saw a gait I recognised, blond hair, a tan that you can only get at altitude and a smile so wide it threatened to break his face.

Like shots from a start gun, Ludo and Iona raced towards him, our Labrador Storm bouncing at their heels, her lead dragging behind her. They dodged the bemused travellers who preceded Ben and leapt into his arms, clinging to their battle-worn father like limpets in a storm.

I held back, not wanting to interfere as my beloved children breathed their father in, touching his beard and examining his face. He put them down and enveloped me into a bear hug, his shaggy beard bristling my face. I scrutinised him closely. His skin was a nut brown, a dark patch of windburn blotting his cheek, his beard greyer than I remembered but his tear-filled brown eyes bore the hallmarks of the man who had missed us as much as we'd missed him.

Having been married 12 years, we should be good at reunions, but I've learned over the last few years that the anticipation, the hope and excitement that you experience in the build-up, puts a lot of pressure on the time you spend together to be perfect, and most of the time perfect is exactly what it's not. What I've learned over the two decades we've been together is to let go of this quest for perfection, to take it slowly and give yourself the time to reconnect.

When someone has experienced such an adventure, when you've not been able to have a conversation for the best part of two months, it's hard to know where to start. And while we wanted to hear all about his adventure, he was also thirsty for what had been going on at home.

While the relative excitement of poetry competitions and the summer fair might seem to pale into insignificance in comparison to climbing Everest, these everyday events make up the rich patchwork of the life that Ben missed so much while he was away. And so we chatted about home life on the way home in the car. Ben heard how Ludo had won a certificate for excellence in swimming and how Iona had been to a party at KidZania, how our naughty dog Storm had eaten my niece's Christening cake and had to go to the vet to have a vomiting injection and that they'd just started watching a new series of Operation Ouch! I knew Everest would be a dialogue that would dominate our conversation for years to come, but it was a story that needed to be told slowly, and in Ben's time.

Returning to royal wedding hysteria having lived a simple and utterly detached life for so long would be weird for anyone, but adding to that the fact that he'd descended nearly 9,000 metres in three days and had yet to sleep in a proper bed must have been quite an extraordinary experience for Ben.

We joined some friends to watch the wedding, drinking rosé and eating pizza in a garden adorned with bunting. Ludo and Iona had continued to cling to their father, as if he might up and leave again should they let go. They inspected his face, felt his beard and drank in his smell, pinching themselves that he was really there.

The next few days were a bit of a blur, the experiences from the roof of the world slowly emerging. I learned a lot of things that Ben had hidden from me: the drama of the exploding oxygen canisters and how sick Victoria had become. Slowly as the weekend unfurled and we lay

*peacefully in the garden or reading to the children before
bed, I started to understand the rawness and visceral beauty
of Everest in a way that the mountain of books I'd read
before had never really conveyed. I loved being around the
Everest oracle, my bearded adventurer who could answer
every question I had about the mountain that had
dominated my childhood dreams. 'Do you have to go
through a gate the marks the beginning of the icefall and
thus an Everest climb?' I asked while we loaded the
dishwasher.*

*In those early days, Ben was definitely not quite all there.
He slept a lot but in spite of my best efforts filling the fridge
with things I knew he loved, he ate sparingly, as if his tummy
was adjusting to a West London diet. But it was more than
that; he spoke more slowly, as if his brain took longer to
compute and hesitated before answering questions. For a
man who speaks, loudly and clearly for a living, the change
was extraordinary.*

*Right from the start, one of the things I was most afraid of
was lasting brain damage, which can be caused by time
spent at extreme altitude. My father had told me how people
cope differently, some acclimatising well and some really
bearing the brunt of time spent above 8,000 metres. They'd
worked out that there was a genetic indicator that could
predict your tolerance and the lasting effect altitude might
have on you. He'd recommended Ben take the test before
Everest, an idea that Ben quickly pooh-poohed. 'If I'm going
to climb Everest, I need to believe I can do it,' he argued, 'I've
got no time for negativity.' I quickly realised that my*

argument that it would be better not to do it at all if you were predisposed to suffer and risk brain damage was not one he wanted to hear, and it was something that haunted me all the time he was up on the mountain.

On my way up to start university aged 18 and shortly after reading Into Thin Air, *I met the boyfriend of a woman who'd been on the mountain in 1996 when the storm hit and was one of the very few to have survived a night in the open air in the death zone. Two years later, he told me that she was never quite the same and that even though she had descended alive, her ability to engage, to articulate her feelings and to empathise was slightly different. Coming back with a pulse was all very well, but at what cost was a question never far from my mind.*

But slowly he has returned, he's adjusted back into the rhythm that our chaotic life ticks along to. Never particularly organised, his forgetfulness still catches him out on a regular basis. We've had to change our front door lock a handful of times and luckily he has two passports. For weeks he sat down to write this book and produced nothing. His tenth book, writing is surely a skill he has by now honed, but the words just wouldn't come out.

I'm not one for apathy, it's all about seizing the moment. 'I'm not sure I can do it,' he moaned one morning. 'I just don't have the words to write this book,' he grumbled. But I couldn't just let him give up and so I told him why he had to document his experiences. I told him how I didn't care about book sales or his advance, how another book on the Ben Fogle shelf of books would mean very little to me. As much as I respected the commitment he'd made to his publishers, I was quite confident there were plenty of other books they'd publish that year. I told him that he owed it to us, not just me and the children, but to the grandchildren I hope will one day fill our lives with joy.

We sacrificed him for two months, but it wasn't just that he wasn't there to be the husband and father that we so desperately rely on. It was the Sunday nights alone, the empty seat beside me at the class assembly, the not knowing when … or if … he'd be back. What do you say to a tearful seven-year-old who between sobs gulps '… but I just miss Daddy so much'?

But, more than that we endured worry and anguish, dark thoughts and heart palpitations. Many a long night I spent tossing and turning, trying to brush away the hellish scenarios that infested my head like a horde of maggots so persistent they depended on me for life. The agonisingly long radio silences while he was up on the mountain, with my friends worrying so much that they hadn't the heart to ask me whether or not I'd heard from him.

What Ben experienced is something that few people have the strength, time, money or resolve to do. But I feel quite strongly that those who are privileged enough to test themselves in the way that Ben did, to push their boundaries to see what is humanly possible and to be forced to reflect on life and what each part, person or experience means to us, have an obligation to share it. Ludo and Iona are small and while they lived and breathed Everest as much as their little lungs could, Lego Ninjago is still as interesting. But one day, they'll read something and realise that not everyone's daddy does that. And maybe one of their children, our grandchildren, will do the same and feel a rush of pride that their grandfather had achieved such a remarkable feat. Stories come alive in the detail but our minds, ever more fragile as we get older, lose that all-important detail. And so that morning, as lines of frustration showed on Ben's mountain-ravaged face, the look of defeat in his eyes, I told him why I refused to let him give up. I will put up with a lot of things, but I won't put up with a book defeating him when the highest mountain on earth hadn't managed that.

THE END

I feel like I've been spat out from the eye of a tornado. Chaos has turned to stunned silence. It is like I am living in a fog. I can still picture the moment of burning bright light on the summit. The lucidity and epiphany. It is there within touching distance, and yet I can't quite reach it.

I have been a little lost since my return. It's not uncommon for people after a long expedition to suffer a form of depression. The excitement and adrenaline of the adventure is brought back to earth with the comparative mundanity of everyday life.

I have experienced it often. Post-expedition blues as I call it. The return to civilian life. It's no surprise that many soldiers experience the same thing after a life of institutionalised warfare and discipline, returning to civvy street with a bump. Many struggle to adapt to the comparative normality of life again.

Expeditions demand resourcefulness and resilience. They keep you on your toes as you are forced to become more creative.

Hunger, thirst, tiredness, exhaustion and discomfort become the norm; everything else is a relief.

Back in the normal world, it's the suffering that is abnormal. Normal life gets flipped on its head and expectations change.

The first time I suffered post-journey blues was when I returned from a year in South America. For a year, I had stimulated my mind with new colours, smells, tastes, sounds, cultures and experiences. For 12 months, my life had burned brightly, like a Bunsen burner, and suddenly I was back to my old life.

I remember vividly sitting in the pub with my friends. Everything was the same. Nothing had changed. Internally, I felt like I had lived a lifetime of experiences. I had found my inner being, and yet all around me was the same. It was discombobulating and confusing. I found it difficult to re-adapt to life. Which was the real life? Which was normal? In my mind, I had experienced such riches, but all around me was sameness.

It was that sameness that felt intolerable. So many people become slaves to normality. They follow society's expectations. Study hard. Get a good job. Get a mortgage and a house. Have a family. Retire. Die. Every part of me wanted to turn my back on this, to set off again and to return to those intoxicating experiences where my mind was constantly stimulated. I wanted to feed my mind.

'But you can't just travel for your whole life,' said a friend, 'you'll have to get a job and earn a living.'

It has always surprised me how man has become a slave to conformity. I don't know if it is instinct or habit. Nature or nurture. Society instils a culture that creates a herd-like mentality in which we are all chasing the same dream.

For the last couple of years, I have travelled the globe for a TV series called *Where the Wild Men Are* in which I've spent time with people, couples and families who have shunned society's 'norms' and gone on to pursue their dreams. Living off the grid in the wilderness, they have decided to search for a simpler, happier life. Let's be honest, life is pretty complicated now. Technology has evolved supposedly to make our lives easier, but in fact it has only made it harder.

Connected to the world 24 hours a day, we have become slaves to technology and information. Our brains work overtime to process information we don't really need. The result is that we move further and further from our natural roots. The wilderness becomes a relic, something to marvel at in a museum.

Expeditions have the same powerful effect. After an intense period of sacrifice and abstinence, it can be a shock to return to gluttony and comfort.

I have often thought that expeditions are like a mirror to the natural world in which care and resourcefulness become a daily part of life. Rationing of resources and respect for your environment become the norm. In urbanised society, we are often so disconnected with the reality of life beyond the cityscape that it can be hard to care. Priorities become warped as we find ourselves driven by cold, hard materialism. The wilderness and natural world become abstract, a place to visit as one would a theme park. Is it any wonder we are so screwed as a species?

It is between these two worlds, gluttony and greed, abstinence and suffering, that I have straddled a lifetime of experiences. I used to find the return overwhelming. I struggled to re-adjust, but the more I experienced, the better accustomed I became. I have always wondered which one was normality.

Coming back from travels to far and distant places is one thing. Returning from a long expedition is another. The first time I had this was when I returned from rowing the Atlantic. For two long months, I had suffered and endured with minimal sleep on the high seas. Life had revolved around a whole new routine of two hours on, two hours off, 24 hours a day.

Water, food and sleep were all luxuries. Solitude and danger had become constant companions. And suddenly I was back in central London. It was overwhelming and the first time I had experienced a real 'low'. Everything felt a little mundane. No one really understood what I had been through.

Although I had learned to deal with these lows, Everest was different. I had walked the narrow line between life and death. I had stared the grim reaper in the eyes. Mortality and immortality. I had lived the fine line between life and death.

Everest had burned so brightly, with such intensity. It had been like a blood transfusion. I felt like my soul had been replaced.

Perhaps it was the spirituality of the experience. I felt like I had been closer to something else. Despite a lifetime of experiences, I felt I had connected on another level. Not in a god-like way but with nature itself. For a short period of time, I had stood where so few had been before me. I had risked my life to walk through a little portal into a parallel world.

I have lived a life of contradictions and parallels, but Everest had been one of the most profound examples of that. On one level, it had been life affirming and brilliantly illuminating and yet I find myself in a perpetual fog.

Perhaps it is the starvation of my brain. For far too many days in the death zone, I restricted the oxygen flowing to my brain. Studies suggest that 12 out of 13 summiteers suffer brain damage. to some degree

My mind has definitely been altered. I am slower. I am more forgetful. I feel calmer and more at peace. Somewhere in the distant corners of my mind I feel is 'me', the person I have been looking for all my life. I feel such pride and contentment at what I have achieved and yet I still feel a little numb, like I am someone else. I sometimes wonder if I left a little of myself on Everest.

Shortly after returning home, I called Victoria to see how she was doing. I hadn't wanted to sound to intense or to gloat, so I had left it a couple of days to allow myself time to re-acclimatise before speaking to her.

'Hey Vic, how are you doing?' I chirped breezily down the phone.

'Not good,' she replied before bursting into tears.

I was shocked. I hadn't realised the profound impact the journey would have on her. Not for once did I ever consider her a failure. Her journey simply had a different ending. Vic had put in more of an effort than any of us, but it was her genetic code that had let her down.

To hear her suffering was heart-breaking. She had come back with a chest infection and the combination of her altitude sickness with ill health and the disappointment of not reaching the summit had colluded to form a perfect storm. She had been diagnosed with clinical depression.

'I feel like I left a part of me on the mountain,' she admitted when I went to see her.

The experience had been as profound for Vic as it had for me. The solitude and power of the mountains had affected her deeply and she was struggling to adapt. Of course, hers was a cocktail of disappointment and regret. For the first time in her life, her body, something she had been able to mould, adapt and control more than almost anyone else on the planet, had let her down. Her experience was nothing to do with her mental or physical aptitude. It was a physiological one.

I felt guilt and remorse. It felt like it was partly my fault that she felt this way. If I hadn't invited her to join me on this expedition, then she wouldn't have crashed.

But then life isn't all about the Hollywood ending. That's probably why I love that Churchill quote, 'Success is stumbling from failure to failure without loss of enthusiasm.'

Life is about light and shade. It is contrasts and colour. Sameness and monotony make us all sheep in a field. What are we if we simply conform to normality? What is normal anyway?

Victoria had shown such resilience and fortitude on Everest. I find her strength and determination inspiring.

The reality is that Victoria hadn't failed. Hers was just a different ending. Of course, it was tinged with disappointment, but the experience for Victoria had been life altering nonetheless.

For Victoria and for me, the journey had been the destination. Together we had climbed endless, soaring peaks across the world. We had been privileged to enter the unique world of mountaineering; to learn new skills and to experience a high-altitude wilderness that few people in the world are lucky enough to see.

The expedition was always about teamwork and I learned a great deal from Vic. It was a unique, life-changing experience that will bond us forever.

We are already planning another adventure, only this one a little closer to sea-level.

As for me, despite a lifetime of experiences I am still at a loss, but I feel like I'm closer than I have ever been to an answer.

Life is about the pursuit of your own dream. You must follow your heart and your soul. There will always be an excuse and reason why you shouldn't. It is so easy to become a slave to the norms, the expectations of society.

The key is to be true to yourself. To be who you are, not what other people want you to be. Individuality is the spice of life. This heady mix can build the spirit and cement the foundations of confidence, and believe me, with confidence you can achieve anything. The confidence of belief and trust in yourself is half the battle. Together they help build an armour to approach life with zest and energy.

When we lost our little boy Willem, I made a promise to live my life brightly. I wanted to embrace opportunity and live it as intensely as I could. As a father, I want to inspire my children to be whoever they want to be, to never be told they can't, won't and shouldn't, and to live a life of dos, cans and will. I have tried to flip a world of negatives into one of positives. I have tried to turn frowns into smiles. Pessimism into optimism.

There is a general assumption that money is the key to happiness. Most people aspire to accumulate finances as a sign of wealth. Society puts a price tag on everything and we often attribute success to wealth.

The material world is built around mankind's desire to accumulate money and to then buy things we don't really need. Materialism and commercialism propagate a kind of one-upmanship. The bigger house, the faster car, the more exotic holiday. You only need to read the newspapers or follow social media to see society's obsession.

Greed and jealousy are the inevitable symptoms whereby we become slaves to the pound or the dollar. Money is king. We worship it. We are blinded to it. We pursue it to the detriment of all else.

For me, the pursuit of experiences is the real wealth of life. I could die having amassed a great fortune, with a huge mansion and an expensive car, but what good is that? Some would argue that you are building your wealth as a legacy to leave your children and their children, but what is the good in that?

Some of the unhappiest people I know are those who have been born into great wealth. Great fortune inhibits ambition and breeds lethargy. If you have everything already, where is the drive and desire?

There are plenty of stories of people who have won the lottery, whose lives have got worse rather than better. Many people find it intolerable to reach the pinnacle of aspirations. When, all your life, you have aspired to become a millionaire, and suddenly, overnight, your ambition is achieved, the only way is down.

A little like the post-expedition blues, life loses a sense of purpose and direction. What do you work towards? Of course there are plenty of examples of those who have turned to philanthropy with their great fortune. Bill Gates doesn't strike me as someone who has lost his ambitious mojo, but for many, the achievement and fruition of their goal can often result in a bit of a let-down.

In my case, it was when you climb the highest mountain and realise the only way is down. But here's the point. It isn't. It's merely the end of one chapter and the beginning of another. Life isn't about the pursuit of a single dream. It isn't about the achievement of one goal. Life is a mixture of so many things.

My life is not about acquiring financial wealth but acquiring experiential wealth. I will not leave my children a vast fortune, but I will leave them a great sum of life experiences, and the attitude that they too should pursue their dreams.

It seems pretty obvious to me that the sum of life is not what we have but who we are. The most interesting people I have met are those who have broken from the shackles of society to pursue their own dreams.

Everest in some ways was the pinnacle of my own aspirations. Nothing about my climb was particularly unique: many others have achieved what I did and the mountain is a far safer and busier place than it was 50 years ago when the likes of Mallory and Irvine sacrificed their lives in the pursuit of ambition and inspiration for a nation coming out of the horrors of war.

But Everest was the culmination of my own romantic dreams. Each individual who stands atop that mountain has their own profound epiphany. For many it is fleeting. For all it is dangerous. For some it is enriching and empowering, and for me it was profoundly life affirming.

My life has never conformed. It has been as unstructured as it has been uncontemporary. Individual and unique, I have always tried to follow my own path, rather than stick to the most well-trodden one.

Uniqueness and individuality can come at a cost. Risk and failure. Sacrifice and discomfort. But with it, come the riches of experience and fulfilment.

I want to live a life full of the riches of happiness and satisfaction. I want to live a life with no regrets. My legacy to my children is to be true to who you are, not what society expects you to be. I want them to know that there will always be more in them. To never give up or give in.

Everest brought me riches beyond my wildest dreams. It was like discovering a treasure chest, the contents of which I am still unpacking. For my family, I hope I will be able to translate and transfer my experience. I hope that it will make me a better father and husband.

Life is so precious. The fragility of our mortality is hidden behind the camouflage of society. In man's effort to harness and tame the wilderness, we have endeavoured to control our very existential being. We have tried to hold back the unstoppable march of time.

Through health and wellbeing, medicine and surgery we have tried to halt the slow march to old age. Through health and safety and risk management we have tried to shield ourselves from the reality of mortality. We do not speak of death. It is the last taboo.

Loss is spoken of in hushed tones. We are frightened to confront it. To admit it. The problem is that denying our own mortality is to forfeit the true engagement of life. By kidding ourselves, we fail to grasp life and make the most of it.

By no means should we live each day in fear of the end, but we are all heading that way, Up.

There's that word again, Up. Upwards. We bury people in the ground, yet I can't help but believe that our souls soar upwards, to somewhere higher.

Man has increasingly become a downward-looking species. Through technological innovation, we have become more inward thinking and downward looking.

Everest reminded me to look Up. To admire life. To confront it. To behold it and to seize it.

On Everest, everything was illuminating. For a fleeting moment, everything made sense. It was like I was given privileged insight behind the scenes of life. For an hour on top of that mountain, I lived in a unique world that is now gone.

As I stood on the roof of the world, I peered down at the world beneath me and I looked Up towards that above me.

Despite the solitude and isolation of that lonely, remote place where so few have stood, I didn't feel alone. I had never been alone. The spirit of my little boy lost was there. Willem had always been there. Watching. Caring. Protecting.

I had never been given the chance to care for him. I had failed to protect him. But he had been my guide and my guardian. I felt his presence. We had done this together. I had fulfilled my own promise to him to live my life and pursue my dreams.

Below was a landscape that reminded me of our relative inconsequentiality on this planet, while above me was the seemingly barren nothingness of what lay ahead.

But through that dark sky shone the bright stars of hope.

Although I had reached the physical finality of the summit, from now on the only way was Up.

EPILOGUE

'Daddy came back! It was so exciting to see him! He smelt of rotten cheese. Storm even knew where we were going! Ludo said, "I almost cried with happiness." I said, "I almost said Yippee!"'

This was Iona's entry in her weekend news diary for school after my return.

As the Irish novelist George A. Moore once said, 'A man travels the world over in search of what he needs and returns home to find it.'

I have been overwhelmed by the tide of warmth and goodwill since coming home. Everest still holds a fascination for millions of people.

One of the most common questions I have been asked since I returned was, 'Is it covered with litter?' As the United Nations' Patron of the Wilderness, one of my roles on the Everest expedition had been to report back on the state of the mountain. I wanted to see for myself, if indeed, Everest was the 'world's highest rubbish dump' as it is so often described.

Between Lukla and the summit of Everest, I was astonished at how little litter I saw. The Nepalese have taken on a huge clean-up campaign in recent years, perhaps to improve their reputation, but also in response to tragic natural disasters. The 2015 earthquake wiped out the Nepalese base camp, not only with a terrible loss of life but also causing an environmental disaster after all the equipment from the climbers was abandoned.

The government implemented a number of requirements for climbers, including that each one bring down 8 kilos of litter, including their own, and incentivised sherpas with $2 per kilo of rubbish removed. They imposed 'litter fines' at Base Camp and tried to address the human faeces problem by encouraging mountaineers like myself to take poo bags up the mountain, as we had indeed done.

The results had been pretty spectacular. I see more rubbish on the rural lanes of Great Britain than I did on the whole mountain trail. When I wrote about my environmental findings in the *Guardian* newspaper, I received a letter a few weeks later.

Dear Ben Fogle, Tashi Dele and Namaste,
I read your article in the Guardian paper. After reading
your article, I felt like I have won a million dollar lottery!
It was such a joy after many depression news from Nepali
news media that it says, litters everywhere in Khumbu
region etc.
　　My name is Ang Dorjee Sherpa and the Chair person for
the Sagarmatha Pollution Control Committee (SPCC) I have

*spent 18 years on Everest region for garbage management
and clean up campaign.*

*I admit that we still have lots more work to do, for
instance recycling the garbage, make frequent clean up
campaign above Camp I on Everest and other mountains.
Your article gave us more strength to make Everest region
beautiful for our future generation.*

*As you said, the Everest region one of the cleanest, tidiest
wilderness trails that you have encountered. The credit goes
to all the people from Khumbu, school teachers, students,
government employees who work in this area, many
mountain climbers and trekkers who love the mountains and
this place.*

Thank You.
Best Regards
Ang Dorjee Sherpa

I loved that letter. The selfless pride and love of the mountains
shines through and I felt honoured to have been able to make a
difference and help tell the world.

Everest has been so many things to me. Fear. Loss. Sacrifice.
Suffering. Beauty. Fulfilment. Ambition. Hope. Inspiration.
Dreams. I hope my story will be a reminder to follow your hopes
and your ambitions and dare to dream. Dream big.

I shall leave my final thoughts for another Ben. My dear friend,
the writer Ben Okri.

Ben wrote me a poem to read on Everest, which I did. It is a
powerful, questioning poem that, a little like my climb, is full of

contradictions, but it seems to sum up the romanticism and the futility of climbing Mount Everest.

Everest by Ben Okri

Some visions
Draw us
To impossible places.
These are visions
That have lived
At the heart of our culture.

They pull us like ants
Up into their white clouds
At the edge of dream.
How many have perished
In the storm or snow?

Their trails are invisible.
Whiteness obliterates
The centuries.
Some visions
Demand only
Our snow-eaten feet
And our ice-broken hands.

Its white stony
Face disdains history.
Into the abyss of its pale mouth
Generations go,
Like sleepwalkers.

Sometimes a single storm blots out
Our elaborate designs.
A civilisation climbs its face
And with a breath is erased again.

But all dreams lead here.
From this lunar height
Everything seems clear:
We must either sit still
Or overcome ourselves.

We are the mountains
We need to climb;
We are our own impossible peak.
Everything that we seek
Is dissolved by fulfilment
And only the trackless path
Is worth travelling.

Some dreams draw us up
Not towards any particular eminence
But to something of which
This mountain is but a mysterious
Symbol, whose meaning eludes us
And ever drives us on, drives us
Up, with the blinding sun in our eyes.

It holds up a mirror
To our fevers and our delirium,
Our hopes and our need to conquer.
There we are shattered
And there we are made.
It is one of the forms of the divine,
Perplexing the riddle of distance.
Is it a call to heroism?
Or to oblivion?

For everyone who ascends
Descends
Into a polar space,
Where the far is near
And the near is farther
Than Valhalla.

Some visions
Draw us
To impossible places
Where breathing
Is a new language
In the wind
And where we can climb
Higher up into the flame of the days
The flower of the streets
The ritual of work
The initiation of sleep
And the simplicity of home.

Because one person did something
Vaguely unthinkable
Considerably impossible,
Because one person did,
Others can till their fields
Or leap to the moon
Dance in a ring of fire
Or walk the treadmill incarnations
Towards the centre of that vast
Invisible rose.

You who climb
And you who sit beneath a tree
And you who at your desk
Await a vision, perhaps an annunciation;
You who scratch at your thoughts
Till your life bleeds

You frozen in fear, or blistered in rage
Singing on an empty stage
You in poverty or in wealth
Some vision draws us on
Which we must follow
Or not be born.

Everest will forever be a part of me.

I hope you too will follow your dreams. Climb your own Everest.

Don't be slaves to conformity. Risk a little. Because without it, you can't live, love or experience. The biggest risk is not taking a risk in the first place. If you take no risks you may avoid defeat, but you can also never really achieve.

Oh, and don't forget to look Up.

OUR CHARITIES

My schoolfriend, Haya Bint Al Hussein, daughter of the late King Hussein of Jordan, created a global movement in memory of her father, Anything is Possible, through which she hoped to inspire people across the world to pursue their dreams and ambitions.

Victoria and I were also keen to work with the British and International Red Cross who had been so vital following the earthquake that devastated Nepal in 2015.

I have long admired the work of the Red Cross and it had been a sobering reminder to see their red and white vehicles in my own London neighbourhood in the aftermath of the Grenfell Tower tragedy. It was a reminder of the life-changing work they do at home and abroad.

Shortly after our first training expedition in Nepal, Victoria and I spent a couple of days with Red Cross Nepal, seeing first hand some of the work they are still doing across the country. We visited a prosthetic centre that worked with men, women and children who had lost limbs in the earthquake and who have been given new artificial limbs.

We met Red Cross volunteers who had lost loved ones in the disaster but who still selflessly and tirelessly work within their communities to ensure their fellow countrymen are prepared in the eventuality of another natural disaster.

It was during the field trip that we witnessed some of the micro-financing work that gives those who lost everything in the disaster the chance to earn an income and a livelihood again.

We also visited a blood bank which was building up a huge reserve of blood in case of another disaster. As a small gesture, I decided to leave a bag of my own blood. I sat in an old chair while a nurse put a tourniquet around my arm and inserted a needle into my vein.

I sat there and watched my blood fill a bag. A wave of dizziness swept over me. I have never been very good with blood, especially my own. Sweat trickled down my brow and my vision started to narrow.

That little bag of blood was the smallest of gestures, but I like to think I left a little of myself for the beautiful Nepalese people. I am honoured to become the first ever ambassador of the British Red Cross.

Finally, through my work with the United Nations as their Patron of the Wilderness, I hoped to use our climb to record the human impact on the mountain. I had heard so many tales of the litter on Everest and I wanted to see it for myself. I wanted to understand the human impact on the precious mountain range and report back to the United Nations on how the mountaineering community can improve their etiquette and minimise their impact on the landscape.

Our work with the Red Cross, Anything is Possible and the United Nations Environment Programme gave me so much motivation during that long climb. Where there was darkness, they were the light.

instagram.com/Anythingispossible

instagram.com/UNEnvironment

instagram.com/BritishRedCross

INDEX

ACKNOWLEDGEMENTS

Climbing a mountain is a solitary challenge but a team exercise. Writing a book is the same. Thanks to everyone who helped create this very personal account of my journey.

Thanks to Iswari Paudel, Garrett Madison and Bhola Paudel.

Thanks to our Climbing Sirdar, Ang Phurba Sherpa.

Thanks to the rope-fixing team: Dendi Sherpa, Pasang Tenjing Sherpa, Siddhi Tamang, Jenjen Lama, Datuk Bhote, Pasdawa Sherpa, Pemba Sherpa, Tenjing Gyalgen Sherpa, Phree Chombi.

Thanks to Deepak Ghimire, Durja Gurung, Lalu Gurung, Bhupal Thapamagar, Khampa Thapamagar and Anish Rai.

Thanks to Kam Dorjee Sherpa who summited with us and to Ang Thindu Sherpa and Ming Dorjee Sherpa for your selfless heroism at giving us your bottles and regulators at one of the most dangerous moments in the whole expedition.

Thanks to my dear friend Princess Haya Bint Al Hussein who helped make this whole adventure possible through the Anything is Possible movement. She has a vision to continue her late father's work to inspire people to believe in themselves and pursue their dreams.

Thanks to Richard Johnson and Nadia Taylor for helping with logistics and to Mark Lucas for your artwork.

Thanks to Myles Archibald, Hazel Eriksson and Alison Menzies at William Collins for believing in my passion and dream and taking a risk on this book. To Martin Toseland, Tom Whiting and Anne Rieley for their keen editorial eyes.

Thanks to Victoria for sharing an incredible journey together. One of the toughest, bravest, boldest people I know. No failures, just different endings.

Thanks to Kenton Cool for guiding Victoria and me through the beautiful world of mountaineering and sharing with us the wonders of the Andes, the Alps and the Himalayas.

Thanks to Mark Fisher for your unwavering happiness. The smile on your face, even through adversity, was inspiring and empowering. Thanks for your beautiful photographs and film-making.

Thanks to Ben Okri for your powerful poem, 'Everest', and for letting us publish it.

Thanks to Jonathan for your companionship (and your daughter) and for keeping us fit and healthy.

Thanks to Neil, Matt and everyone at CNN for sharing our journey from afar.

Thanks to Charlie Morison and Jo Calam at Campbell Bell Communications for all your help.

Thanks to Dr Sundeep Dhillon and the team at the Institute of Sport, Exercise and Health for all your help and advice.

Thanks to Philippa and Jacqui for logistics and packing, and to Alex and Derek Adams for being my biggest supporters and looking after Mum when she was ill.

Thanks to Marina, my heroine. While I am away, Marina is the one who runs the family. You are the glue that keeps us together when we are apart. My rock, without you I would be half the person I am. While adventure might be in my blood, it is you that makes me, me. You complete me. You have always allowed me to be the person I am. I may have been the one to stand on the roof of the world but it was a true team effort and you were there too.

Finally, this book is dedicated to Ludo and Iona. You are my world. My life. My everything. This book is for you. I hope you will both grow up with no ceilings or boundaries. I hope that you have the curiosity and determination to pursue your own adventures and dreams.